The Evidence Camera

EasyTech Series

The Evidence Camera

Deanne C. Siemer

Frank D. Rothschild

National Institute for Trial Advocacy

Siemer, Deanne C., Frank D. Rothschild, *The Evidence Camera* (NITA 2004)

ISBN 1-55681-783-5

Library of Congress Cataloging-in-Publication Data pending

TABLE OF CONTENTS

ACKNOWLEDGMENTS

Acknowledgments with respect to using an evidence camera in the courtroom must start with Sam Solomon who pioneered the use of this and other technology. Sam, the founder and CEO of DOAR Communications, Inc., came across an evidence camera in the late 1980s and immediately understood its utility for trial lawyers. Sam's company began to sell evidence cameras and in the early 1990s started equipping federal and state courtrooms with improved evidence cameras, including design features that were the result of his feedback to the manufacturer. Sam has made a great contribution to the techniques reported in this book, and to the work of the authors.

The page design was done by Jude Phillips and edited by Ann Jacobson. The production of the book was coordinated by Shelly Goethals. The authors are also indebted to everyone who worked on *Effective Use of Courtroom Technology: A Lawyer's Guide to Pretrial and Trial* (NITA 2002) and *Easy Tech: Cases and Materials on Courtroom Technology* (NITA 2001), from which some materials in this book are drawn.

SEND US YOUR COMMENTS

We would like to hear from you! Visit the NITA website at *www.nitastudent.org* and tell us what you like about the book or what should be changed in the next edition. We are glad to get new ideas to be exchanged within the NITA family.

ABOUT THE AUTHORS

 Deanne C. Siemer is a trial lawyer from Washington, DC who has specialized in commercial cases in federal and state courts, and who has tried large contracts, business torts, and patent cases using courtroom technology. She serves as a court-appointed arbitrator and mediator, teaches courses in trial practice and courtroom technology, and consults on case theory and presentation in trial cases.

 Frank D. Rothschild has tried civil cases in private practice and criminal cases as a public defender and state prosecutor. He currently holds an appointment as a local court judge in Kauai, Hawaii, and serves professionally as a mediator and arbitrator. He teaches courses in trial practice and courtroom technology, and provides training for judges and law firms and consults on trial cases.

OTHER NITA TECHNOLOGY BOOKS

Effective Use of Technology: A Lawyer's Guide to Pretrial and Trial, by Deanne Siemer with Donald H. Beskind, Anthony J. Bocchino, and Frank D. Rothschild (NITA 2002). Outlines uses and objections with respect to all forms of technology found in federal (and increasingly in state) courtrooms.

Effective Use of Technology: A Judge's Guide to Pretrial and Trial, a joint project of the Federal Judicial Center and NITA. Distributed to all federal district court judges, bankruptcy judges, and magistrate judges.

PowerPoint 2002 for Litigators, by Deanne Siemer and Frank Rothschild (NITA 2002). Uses a demonstration case file with fourteen digital exhibits, including video and audio clips as exhibits, and illustrates step-by-step how to create all types of litigation exhibits for use at trial.

PowerPoint for Litigators, by Deanne Siemer and Frank Rothschild, with Edward R. Stein and Samuel H. Solomon, (NITA 2000). Covers PowerPoint 2000 and PowerPoint 97; uses three case files—criminal, civil, and personal injury—with digital exhibits.

Basic PowerPoint Exhibits, by Deanne Siemer and Frank Rothschild (NITA 2003). Part of the EasyTech series of small handbooks; describes step-by-step how to create bullet point, photo, and document exhibits.

Argument Slides, by Deanne Siemer and Frank Rothschild (NITA 2003). Part of the EasyTech series; describes how to make weight of the evidence slides, relationship charts, yes-no checklists, decision trees, relative merit charts, illustrated time lines, and attack slides.

Guide for Teaching PowerPoint for Litigators, by Deanne Siemer and Frank Rothschild (NITA 2000). A short outline of how to present a three-hour course on constructing basic exhibits with PowerPoint 2000.

Corel Presentations for Litigators, by Deanne Siemer and Frank Rothschild (NITA 2000). Provides instructions on making litigation exhibits with the Corel WordPerfect software suite.

Easy Tech: Cases and Materials on Courtroom Technology, by Deanne Siemer, Frank Rothschild, and Anthony J. Bocchino (NITA 2001). Materials for classroom teaching in law schools and in NITA programs on the use of basic technology—laptop computers, evidence cameras, and telestrators.

Demonstration: Presentation Technology in the Courtroom, Deanne Siemer, Frank Rothschild, and Samuel H. Solomon (NITA 2000). Provides a script and ready-made exhibits for demonstrating the use of the evidence camera, laptop computer, and telestrator in a trial setting.

PREFACE

This EasyTech Guide focuses on using an evidence camera in the courtroom. This equipment is known by a number of generic and trade names, among them document camera, object display camera, document imager, visualizer, visual presenter, DOAR presenter, and Elmo. All refer to the same thing. The evidence camera is often a starting point for lawyers who are incorporating technology into their presentations. It is simple to operate, reliable in performance, and effective in presentation.

At its foundation, courtroom technology is a means for putting evidence before everyone in the courtroom—the judge, the jurors, the opposing lawyers, the courtroom support staff, and even onlookers—at the same time. The displays, usually on monitors or projection screens, convey many kinds of information more efficiently. Most lay people can look at a display and follow along with an explanation more readily than they can find the place in a hard copy document and read the small type while also trying to listen.

The evidence camera methods and techniques explained in this Guide are generic types that have wide applicability for all kinds of civil and criminal cases. The explanation covers the setup and use of the equipment, presentation of various categories of evidentiary exhibits and illustrative aids, and integration into presentations that also use other equipment such as laptop computers and PowerPoint displays.

Hardware required: This Guide focuses on the basic evidence camera sold by a number of litigation support companies and manufacturers (listed in chapter 12). The evidence camera requires a means of displaying its output—usually a digital projector and screen, but sometimes digital monitors (described in chapter 3). It does not require any computer equipment, although evidence cameras are sometimes used in conjunction with a laptop computer.

Knowledge required: This Guide is self-contained. You do not need any knowledge of electronics, video cameras, or cabling beyond what is explained here. The basic uses of the evidence camera involve no software or knowledge of computers.

Other resources: For more details on this and other types of courtroom technology, see *Effective Use of Courtroom Technology: A Lawyer's Guide to Pretrial and Trial* (NITA 2002), and *Easy Tech: Cases and Materials on Courtroom Technology* (NITA 2001).

Chapter 1: Introduction to the Evidence Camera

This chapter introduces the evidence camera for those who have not yet seen this equipment. Readers who are familiar with the evidence camera in general can turn to chapters 2 through 8 for specific materials about uses in the courtroom.

1.1 What is it?

An evidence camera is a relatively simple device that combines a stationary video camera and adjustable lighting to create a "live" image.

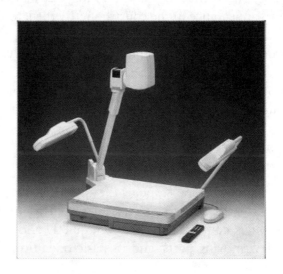

"Evidence camera" is a name often used in the legal setting. Elsewhere, this equipment is known as

- Document camera
- Document imager
- Object display camera
- Visualizer
- Visual presenter
- Portable image input device
- DOAR Presenter, Elmo (and other commercial trade names)

Evidence cameras have been around for a long time. The use of courtroom technology began in the 1970s when slide projectors, overhead projectors, and videotape players made appearances in trials. Document cameras and object display devices were already being used in corporate settings, for meetings and training, but had not yet made an appearance in the courtroom. By the late 1980s, evidence cameras were in use by a few lawyers, replacing overhead projectors, and in the early 1990s, evidence cameras were often seen in larger trials. When federal courtrooms began to be equipped with technology in the mid 1990s, evidence cameras were almost always included. State courts followed suit. Almost any court that has some technology capability has an evidence camera of some kind.

The evidence camera is one of the easiest and least finicky devices for a lawyer to use in a courtroom. Once turned on, it continues to function, quietly and reliably. It has few moving parts, and its basic operation can be mastered within minutes.

1.2 What does it do?

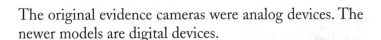

The stationary video camera works like any other video camera. When it is on, it generates an image of anything within the focal length of the lens. The video camera is mounted on a stand, so that anything put on the base under the camera, so long as the power is on, will result in an image that can be captured, transmitted, enlarged, and displayed for viewing in a courtroom setting.

Like other video cameras, the evidence camera has a zoom capability, so that the user can enlarge the view of a particular part of a document or feature of an object that has been placed under the camera.

1.3 Basic types

The original evidence cameras were analog devices. The newer models are digital devices.

Analog means electronic transmission using signals of varying frequency or amplitude. Television sets, standard telephone sets, assisted listening headsets, video conferencing equipment, video monitors, standard video cameras, VCR's, and video and audio tape players are analog equipment.	**Digital** means electronic transmission using discrete units (ones and zeros). Computers, CD players, DVD players, digital cameras, computer monitors, computer printers, and projectors that operate with computers are digital equipment.

The most significant thing one needs to know about the difference between analog and digital equipment is that they are compatible only with a converter. Otherwise, analog equipment cannot transmit successfully to digital display devices, and digital equipment cannot transmit successfully to analog display devices. Converters are often built into evidence cameras and the projectors or monitors on which their output is displayed.

A principal advantage of digital equipment over analog equipment is higher resolution. A good digital evidence camera can make a whole page of a document readable on the screen; generally an analog evidence camera must zoom in on a part of the document in order to make it readable. In addition, digital equipment generally has better zoom (enlargement) capability and better remote controls. Digital equipment can also store and recall images.

1.4 Basic setup

Evidence cameras do not work alone. They need some type of display device. The evidence camera is cabled to the display device and the image generated by the evidence camera is shown on the display device.

The earliest evidence cameras transmitted analog images to video (television) monitors, just as other video cameras did. Courtrooms often had video (analog) monitors in order to play videotapes of depositions or events or facilities at issue. Most new evidence cameras still have the capability to display images on video monitors because they have built-in converters for this purpose.

The newer evidence cameras transmit analog or digital images to digital (computer) monitors or to a digital projector and projection screen. The evidence camera is cabled to the projector, and the projector uses a bright light source and powerful lens to throw the enlarged image to the projection screen.

Some courtroom setups have one or more large monitors outside the jury box and all the jurors are looking at the same monitor. Other courtrooms have built small monitors into the jury box in configurations where typically two jurors share a monitor. In this kind of setup, the evidence camera is cabled to the central connection for the courtroom display system, and from that connection, cables run to the monitors. Anything put on the evidence camera is then displayed on all the connected monitors.

1.5 Alternative uses

An evidence camera is an image generator. In a courtroom setting, it can work as the only image generator or it can be combined with other methods of displaying evidence. Using the evidence camera in conjunction with other technology is explained in chapter 10.

A digital evidence camera may have capability in addition to generating images. Good digital equipment can capture an image of an object or other material in front of its lens and transmit that image to a laptop computer for storage or to a VCR for recording on tape. It also may have the capability to accept input from a laptop computer (such as a PowerPoint slide show), a VCR (excerpts from deposition tapes), or a digital camera and coordinate the courtroom presentation seamlessly.

Chapter 2: Evidence Camera Equipment

The evidence camera has five components: (1) a video camera; (2) an arm that positions the camera over its base; (3) lighting; (4) cabling; and (5) controls. The evidence camera is about 18 to 20 inches square and weighs 10 to 20 lbs. It has no special mounting requirements. The unit will sit on any table or other level surface. The evidence camera is usually completely portable. It folds up into a convenient carrying case, and travels well because it has almost no moving parts.

> This section uses common equipment as a model in showing the component parts. There are small variations from manufacturer to manufacturer, and the labels on some of the equipment may be slightly different. The manufacturers and current models are described in chapter 12.

2.1 Video camera

The video camera portion of the equipment has only a few parts: a standard camera, a closeup lens (on some models), and controls for the camera (discussed in section 2.5 below).

Camera

The video camera, while optimized for this particular application, is much like any other video camera. It generates a video image of anything within the range of its lens.

Lens

The camera lens on most evidence cameras is optimized for focus on paper or transparencies lying flat on the base. Evidence cameras are also designed to provide excellent focus for small objects placed on the base. Some specialized units (usually called object display cameras) have lenses that provide exceptional clarity for three-dimensional objects. The lens on all types of evidence cameras provides for close-up views using a zoom capability.

In older units, the camera has an external closeup lens which must be on when the camera is aimed down at its base, and must be off when the head is rotated to the front or back to focus on something at a distance. Most newer cameras do not include a removable closeup lens as almost all uses involve the lens in the standard downward-facing position.

Lens cap

The camera lens is protected by a lens cap that needs to be removed before the unit is operated.

2.2 Arm

◆

The video camera is mounted at the top of an arm, usually retractable, which is connected to the base of the unit. When the unit is ready for operation, the arm is upright, stretched to its full length, and locked into position. The arm's locked position puts the camera at the correct height above the base.

The arm has a rotating connection for the camera so that it can point down at anything on the base below it or outward at anything in front of it. Some cameras can also turn from side to side while pointed out and away from the base.

A retractable arm has two release buttons. A release button on the side of the arm near the top retracts the arm so that it fits within the footprint of the base. A release button next to the point where the arm joins the based folds the arm from its upright position onto the base.

Video camera

Retractable arm

Wing light

Base light

Controls

2.3   Lighting

◆

The evidence camera works well in natural light, and most black and white exhibits need no additional light.

For special exhibits, the evidence camera comes with two light sources: high intensity overhead lights above the base, and a back light contained in the base. Each set of lights (the one in the base and the two in the arms) has a separate on/off switch; in normal operation, both sets of lights are off.

Wing/upper lights

The wing or upper lights usually have bright fluorescent bulbs and are used to increase the contrast when presenting materials in color.

These lights may also be used when the normal lighting in the courtroom is not adequate to produce a good image.

A button on the front panel turns these lights on and off but, when the button is pressed, the lights do not come on immediately. There is a short 5–10 second warmup period and then the lights come on.

The arms holding these lights allow adjustment of the angle of each light; and the arms fold down onto the base when the unit is packed for travel.

Back light

The back light is used when light needs to come up through the material being presented—such as an X-ray or a transparency.

The back light cannot be used when the wing or upper lights are on.

2.4 Cabling

The evidence camera has one power cord and one cable to connect to the display device, usually a monitor or projector. The setup for the evidence camera in the courtroom is discussed in chapter 3.

Connection (rear) panel

The connections for power and display are on the rear panel of the base. The panel usually looks something like this.

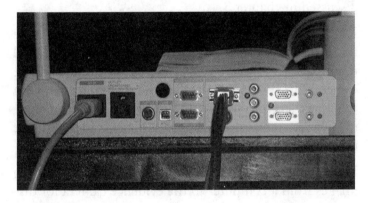

Power cord

The rear panel of the evidence camera has an "AC in" and sometimes an "AC out" connection. The power cord is plugged into the "AC in" connection on the evidence camera and into the AC outlet in the courtroom. (The "AC out" connection is used when another device is plugged into the evidence camera as a source of power.)

The power cord for most evidence cameras is about six feet long, making an extension cord a standard part of the equipment kit for courtroom use. The power cord is usually detachable from the unit for easier packing.

For courtroom use, it is recommended that the power cord be plugged into a surge protector, and the surge protector, in turn, be plugged into a standard three-prong wall outlet.

Most newer evidence cameras have adapters allowing use within foreign electrical systems with voltage different from the U.S. system.

Display cable

Most evidence cameras are set up to deal with several outputs and inputs. The projectors and monitors to which the evidence camera may be hooked up are discussed in chapter 3.

RGB output: The "RGB out" connection is used to cable the evidence camera to a digital projector or a digital monitor. Connect one end of the cable to the evidence camera's "RGB out" connection and the other end of the cable to the projector's or the monitor's "RGB in" connection. A standard RGB cable usually comes with the unit.

RGB input: The "RGB in" connection is used to bring images from a computer to the evidence camera for display through the evidence camera. Some models use a USB connection for this purpose.

Video (or S-video) output: The "video out" connection is used to cable the evidence camera to the "video in" connection on a video (analog) monitor, a television set, or a VCR. Standard commercially-available video cable is used for this purpose. This kind of cable usually does not come with the unit. (Note: when connecting to a video monitor or a VCR, you need to pay attention to whether these units are NTSC or PAL format.)

Video (or S-video) input: The "video in" connection is used to receive input from a VCR, a digital still camera, or a digital video camera.

RS 232C input: This is usually used when you want to control the evidence camera from a computer rather than from the evidence camera's own control panel or from a remote control.

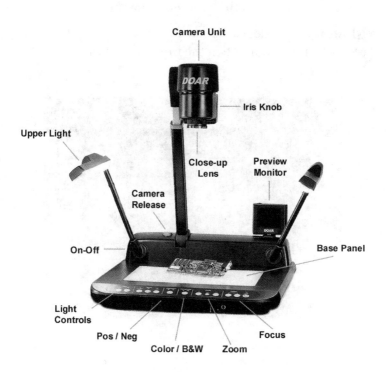

2.5 Controls

◆

The evidence camera has very few controls, and all are very intuitive to operate. The evidence camera can be controlled from the panel on its base, from a remote, or from a laptop computer. The operation of these controls is explained in chapter 4.

2.5.1   Controls on the evidence camera

Most of the evidence camera's controls are located on a control panel mounted on the front of the base. It usually looks like this.

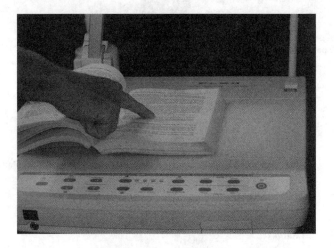

On-off

Most evidence cameras have an on-off switch, usually placed at the side of the unit. Some models, however, need only to be plugged into a standard electrical outlet as a power source. When you plug it in and turn it on, the camera is activated. It stays activated until you turn it off or unplug it from the power source.

Focus

Like any camera, the evidence camera needs to be focused in order to display a crisp, clear image. It usually has three focus buttons: two manual controls and one automatic control.

Manual focus is needed for any three-dimensional object because of the different depths of field presented by the object. The manual focus is operated by two buttons labeled "N" (near) and "F" (far).

Autofocus is most useful with documents, photographs, and other exhibits that lie flat on the base. It is operated by a single button located next to the manual focus buttons. Press it once, and it figures out where to focus.

Zoom (enlargement)

The zoom feature on the evidence camera is like the zoom on a 35 mm camera or video camera. It allows the operator to change the focus of the lens to make the field of vision smaller and to enlarge every detail being viewed.

The zoom in button enlarges the image. This is a continuous action button, so that the person operating the evidence camera presses and holds down the zoom in (sometimes called "tele") until the amount of enlargement is sufficient, then stops pressing the button.

The zoom out button (sometimes called "wide") does just the opposite. To retreat from an enlargement and get back to normal size, the person operating evidence camera presses the zoom out button and holds it down until the right level of enlargement is reached; then the button is released.

Freeze

This button freezes the image being transmitted so that the exhibit can be taken off the evidence camera and a new exhibit put on it without any change in the image on the screen. This avoids eye-jarring motion when exhibits are put on and taken off the evidence camera.

Memory

This control stores the image currently being transmitted by the camera (up to six or eight images) which can later be recalled to the screen exactly as they were when they were stored and without the object or document that was on the base of the evidence camera when the image was stored.

Iris (brightness or exposure)

Most evidence cameras have manual and automatic iris controls which darken or lighten the image.

The manual control is a knob located on the camera head. Generally the setting is kept in the middle.

The auto control is governed by an internal mechanism that will adjust for the best contrast under most circumstances.

Black & white

Color images can be turned to black and white by using the black & white switch. In older evidence cameras, the black & white switch is on for normal operation with documents.

Color

The color switch activates an automated enhancement for color images. If the camera is aimed at something that has color in or on it, the color switch should be on. In newer cameras, the color switch can be left on at all times unless it is necessary to change a color image to black and white. There is no longer a discernible difference in image quality when displaying text documents in the color mode vs. the black and white mode.

Lights

The base light has an on-off switch.

The wing or upper lights have a separate on-off switch.

Positive/negative

On some evidence cameras there is a special switch for using photographic negatives and X-rays.

In normal operation, the positive/negative switch is set to positive.

When the negative switch is on, and there is a photographic negative or X-ray on the base, the image shown is a reproduction of the negative. When the positive switch is on, the negative is turned to a positive image.

2.5.2 Remote control

A wireless remote control unit is supplied with most digital evidence cameras. If you use a remote, remember to have a set of spare batteries handy, and always change batteries before starting trial.

You need to know where the remote control sensor is located on the evidence camera so that you can point the remote at it. Sometimes this sensor is in the camera head; other models put it in the base.

The remote control will specify its range, and you need to be sure to stay within it. The range is usually about 15 feet from the evidence camera; 100 degrees around the sensor; and 30 degrees up or down from the sensor. This means that if you are using a remote, the placement of the evidence camera is important.

The buttons on the remote control replicate the buttons on the front control panel of the base. Each manufacturer's remote is a little different, so you will need to study the placement of the buttons and practice using the remote to display the exhibits you will be using.

Some remote controls include a "finger pointer" that puts a graphic of a pointing finger on the image which can be moved by clicking arrows on the remote to point out a particular feature on the screen. Other remotes include a laser pointer which puts a small red dot on the screen that can be moved by tilting or waving the remote. Neither of these features are particularly useful in litigation contexts.

2.5.3 Computer controls

Most digital evidence cameras also allow operation from a laptop computer. All of the controls on the base of the evidence camera are replicated on the display on the laptop's monitor. This allows the coordination of displays using a number of technologies. See chapter 10.

Chapter 3: Projectors, Monitors, and Courtroom Setup

An evidence camera generates an image that is transmitted to a display device. In a courtroom, the usual display devices are a digital projector and screen or digital monitors. This chapter explains each of these display options and shows some basic courtroom layouts.

3.1 Digital projector and screen

The easiest, cheapest, and most reliable setup for an evidence camera is to connect it to a digital projector which, in turn, displays your images on a blank wall or a single large 6, 8, or 10-foot screen. This makes the lowest demands on the technical skill of the person who does the courtroom setup. The direct connection between the evidence camera and the projector offers the least complexity and the lowest opportunity for failure.

Two types of digital projectors are used in courtrooms: fixed and portable.

A fixed installation projector is usually owned by the court. It has been installed in a wall or ceiling to be unobtrusive and can be covered when not in use.

A portable projector is usually provided by one of the parties. These units are relatively inexpensive to buy, but can also be rented at most good audio visual supply stores.

The projector should have sufficient lighting power to put clear images on the projection screen without dimming any courtroom lights. Lighting power is measured in lumens, and a projector with a rating of 1,000 lumens or more is needed. The requirements for lighting power vary with the distance between the projector and the screen. Permanent installations in which the projector is quite far from the screen require more lighting power (and a higher lumens rating). Temporary installations in which the projector and screen are only 10 to 20 feet apart produce very clear images with only 1,000 lumens.

The projector should also have a quiet fan (needed to dissipate heat) so that no distracting noise accompanies its operation.

Most newer digital projectors have built-in converters so they can display the output from analog (VHS video, analog evidence cameras) as well as digital devices.

Digital projectors are designed to accept incoming data at a particular resolution. This refers generally to the amount of information to be displayed at one time by the projector. The resolution of the projector and the input device must match, otherwise the projector cannot display the image. A mismatch is not usually a difficult problem to overcome. If the resolution of the evidence camera is higher than that of the projector, there is usually a control on the evidence camera that allows it to decrease its output to match that of the projector. If the resolution of the projector is higher than that of the evidence camera, there is a control on most projectors that allows it to match the input device.

Screen

The projection screen is normally a 6-foot by 8-foot unit or an 8-foot by 10-foot unit. It can be wall mounted (pulled down as needed) or stand mounted (folded up when not needed). In some courtrooms, the projection screen is recessed into the ceiling and retracts when not in use. The screen should be matte white and its surface should be specially treated (ultra-reflective high gain) to reflect light efficiently. A screen used in a fully lighted courtroom needs to provide about 50 percent more brightness than a conventional projection screen designed for video or slide shows done under dimmed lighting conditions.

3.2 Digital monitors

Three types of digital monitors are used in courtrooms.

CRT monitor

A cathode ray tube (CRT) is a specialized vacuum tube in which images are produced when an electron beam strikes a phosphorescent surface. The CRT in a computer monitor is similar to the picture tube in a television receiver. CRT monitors are large and heavy. The tube requires a boxy or oblong shape; the larger the screen, the longer the box. CRT monitors are the least expensive alternative, and they are generally highly reliable.

Most CRT monitors have a slightly concave surface. Newer models have a flat surface which reduces glare and is a better option for courtroom use. They are known as "flat-screen" monitors (not to be confused with "flat-panel" monitors which are LCD monitors described below.)

LCD monitor

Liquid crystal display (LCD) technology allows monitors to be much thinner than CRT technology. An LCD is constructed with a grid of conductors with a pixel located at each intersection in the grid. A current is sent across two conductors in the grid to control the light for any pixel. These monitors are also known as "flat-panel displays." This technology, in high-quality equipment, produces image clarity that is as good or better than a CRT monitor.

One problem with flat panels is that they need to be viewed fairly straight on because all the liquid crystals are directed toward the front of the display. If the viewer is too much to one side, the picture loses contrast and the lines may appear grainy. For this reason, flat panels are usually constructed so they can be rotated 90 degrees on their base.

There are several ways to provide wider angle viewing. The least expensive involves adding a diffuser film to the top layer of the display, which redirects the light coming out of the panel so that it leaves the screen in all directions. Inplane switching (IPS) technology changes the path that the electricity takes through the liquid crystal layer which results in an increased viewing angle. This diminishes brightness to some extent. Multidomain vertical aligned (MVA) technology uses special liquid crystal materials that produce an increased viewing angle without sacrificing brightness.

LCD monitors come in two main types: active matrix and passive matrix. The active matrix is faster and more colorful, but also more expensive.

§3.2

Plasma monitor

A plasma monitor creates images by running electricity through superheated gas. It is a large flat panel video display, which generates its own light, offering film quality images through a palette of 16.7 million colors.

Plasma technology automatically resizes and focuses input from computers, VCRs, and television broadcasts. It has a viewing angle of 160 degrees horizontally and vertically enabling an excellent view from all points in the jury box.

Plasma units are only 3 to 6 inches deep, so they can be mounted on a wall or a floor stand. They are now available in screen sizes that range from 37 inches to 50 inches; the most popular size is 42 inches. These monitors weigh from 65 to 100 pounds. The native resolution of most plasma monitors is 852 x 480, but some of the newer models offer 1280 x 768.

3.3. Courtroom setup

The setup for the courtroom is highly dependent upon the physical layout of the court and the limitations imposed by the judge. This section provides some general guidance.

3.3.1 Setup with projector and screen

A setup using a digital projector and screen in a courtroom requires quite a lot of room, which may not be available in smaller courtrooms. It also is best used in a configuration in which the screen is set up opposite the jury box, so the jury can take in the displays and the lawyer has enough maneuvering room to be able to walk up to the screen to point out particular information, if necessary. Some courtrooms cannot accommodate this layout.

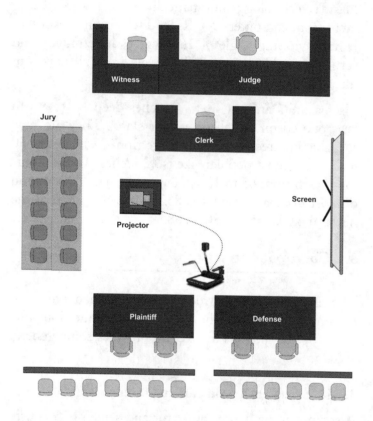

There is an additional benefit if the screen can be located fairly near the witness, so that the jury can see the witness and the screen easily, and so the witness can come down off the stand and point things out. However, in most courtrooms, the witness stand is on the same side of the judge as the jury, on the theory that the witness should be as close to the jury as possible. Under those circumstances, the screen will be some distance from the witness.

A projector demands considerable space in a courtroom. If possible, you want your screen located straight across from the jury box. You need about twice the distance from the first row of seats as the size of the screen. A 6-foot screen will be about 12 feet from the audience; an 8-foot screen will be about 16 feet away; and a 10-foot screen needs about 20 feet. Most experts think that the 8-foot or 10-foot screen is the best choice. As a practical matter, you need a high ceiling and an area 35 to 40 feet wide and 40 to 50 feet deep to use a 10-foot screen effectively.

Courtroom lighting can present a problem when using a projection screen. If there are lights immediately over the screen, the image will wash out on the screen. Other lights usually do not affect an image on a projection screen so long as the projector has sufficient power. If the problem cannot be solved by moving the screen, the few lights that cause the problem can be handled (with the permission of the court clerk) by temporarily loosening the bulb or taping cardboard over the fixture.

Positioning the projector: The projector needs a stable table, tripod, or stand. If it wobbles, the image on the screen will wobble. Correct height is important to get a good image on the screen. The projector should be at a height sufficient to point directly at the center of the screen. When the projector is pointed up at the screen, there will be a keystone effect in which the top of the image is wider than the bottom. Most digital projectors have anti-keystone controls to reduce this effect, but they correct only relatively small upward angles.

Positioning the evidence camera: The evidence camera also needs a stable table or cart, usually in a different location from the projector. An unstable surface may cause the evidence camera to fall on the floor, which can break the bulbs and lens. The height of the table makes no difference to the image on the screen, but the equipment should be at a height that makes it easy to put exhibits on and off the evidence camera. The table should be small enough so that it is easy to get close to the evidence camera for moving exhibits on and off the base.

If there is a lectern in the courtroom from which the lawyers address the court, the witnesses, and the jury, the evidence camera normally is placed on a small table to one side of the lectern.

If there are counsel tables but no lectern, the evidence camera may be located on a small table between counsel tables. The camera is usually shared equipment that both sides will use, and it needs to be in a place convenient for both lawyers.

Normally when a witness uses the evidence camera, he or she comes down from the witness stand to the equipment. Occasionally an existing courtroom setup will have an evidence camera on a small table at the witness stand as well.

3.3.2 Setup with monitors

There are two typical setups when the court has already installed monitors. As large plasma monitors become more practical, many courts have them outside the jury box. In earlier installations, courts usually opted to install small LCD monitors inside the jury box.

In either case, the court will have non-jury monitors for the judge, counsel, witness, and key courtroom staff. Small flat-panel LCD monitors are usually used at the bench, at the witness stand, at a lectern, and on counsel table where space is a premium. A 15-inch display is adequate at close distances.

Large monitors outside jury box

Large plasma monitors are usually used when the jury's monitors are outside the jury box in the well of the courtroom. The minimum size depends on the distance from the jurors, but 42 inch monitors or larger are usually

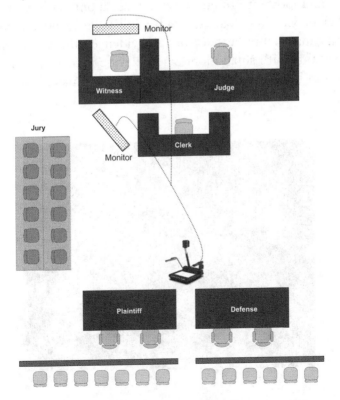

required. Large monitors may be used behind the witness stand to display videotapes and videoconferences of witness testimony.

Small monitors inside jury box

Some courtrooms have small flat panel monitors installed in the jury box, usually one for every two jurors. This setup makes the courtroom less cluttered. Some judges believe it also increases efficiency because any digital input equipment can be plugged into the connection at the lectern, and all the displays light up. With a monitor in front of each two chairs in the jury box, each juror has almost exactly the same viewing angle, which is not true when large monitors outside the jury box are used.

One important limitation with small monitors is insufficient viewing space to read a full page of documentary material projected from an evidence camera. When working with small monitors, the evidence camera must zoom in on a particular part of a page to make it readable.

Small monitors also present a special challenge because of the tendency to lose group focus, especially during an opening statement or closing argument. Jurors look down at the monitor instead of out into the courtroom at the advocate. When jurors are looking down, they may be paying attention only peripherally to what the advocate is saying or doing. If the message is in what is being said, they may miss most of it. The lawyer loses the ability to communicate directly with the jurors as compared to the setting where the display is in the same view as the lawyer as is the case when using a large projection screen. This communication style can be very effective —in part because it is used by television commentators and thus is within the experience of virtually every juror. It is also a more familiar setting as most trial lawyers are accustomed to working in front of large exhibits on easels and using them as a means of drawing attention to information.

Timing, communication style, and presentation skills are much more important when the lawyer is using small monitors. Lawyers can control the "look down" factor by putting black slides into their presentations at appropriate points or using a software control that blanks the screen. The lawyer has to pause, blank the screen to get the jury to look back at the lawyer, and then go on.

Chapter 4: Operating the Evidence Camera Equipment

Basic operation of the evidence camera involves a short checklist for starting up the equipment, a few pointers about placing documents or objects on the base of the evidence camera, and the procedures for zooming in and out in order to enlarge the image when necessary.

4.1 Startup

Open the unit and get it ready to operate.

- Place the evidence camera on a stable table or cart at a height convenient for placing exhibits on the camera's base. The camera can be at any height as its placement has nothing to do with the image on the screen.

- Unfold the wing or upper lights

- Press the arm lock release button at the base of the retractable arm and raise the arm until it is fully extended and locks into place.

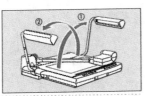

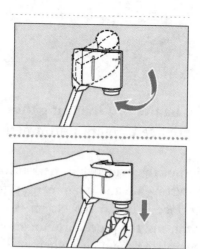

- Rotate the camera head so that its lens is pointing down toward the base.

- Remove the lens cap.

- Make sure the close-up lens is on (if manually attached) or switched on (if built in).

- Check out the equipment when it is in place in the courtroom where it will be used well in advance of displaying the first exhibit.

- Check the power connection for the evidence camera. The power cord should be plugged into the back of the evidence camera and into a surge protector on the other end. The surge protector should be plugged into the wall. Make sure you have extra three-prong to two-prong plug adapters in case the courtroom outlet takes only two-pronged plugs.

- Check the power connections for the display devices. Projectors and monitors that are brought to the courtroom for a particular trial (and are not part of the courtroom's regular equipment) should be connected to the surge protector as well.

- Tape the power cords to the floor to avoid tripping over the cords and toppling the equipment. Gaffing tape (not duct tape) is useful for this as it does not leave a residue on the floor or carpet.

- Turn on the display device. Some projectors and monitors need to be turned on before the evidence camera is turned on in order that they can adequately detect the incoming signal.

- Turn on the evidence camera.

- Put a test pattern on the evidence camera base in order to focus the camera.

- Turn on the wing or upper lights if the room lights are not adequate to get a good image on the screen.

4.2 Placement of exhibits

Documents should be placed on the evidence camera base so that the entire document is visible on the screen when the evidence camera is zoomed out to its farthest setting. The document camera may have document positioning markers along the edges of the base. If not, it is useful to put small pieces of tape along the edge of the base to mark the proper placement of a document.

The video camera picks up the image of a document exactly as the eye sees it, so the top of the document should be at the top of the base.

If the exhibits to be displayed include documents, place a large piece of black construction paper on the base of the evidence camera covering the white rectangle for the base light. A black rubber piece can also be used for this purpose. Even with the base light off, white documents do not display well on a white background. The cover eliminates the white glare from the base. White on white makes documents hard to look at and also creates a somewhat "unreal" image because the document looks like text floating on a large white background rather than a defined page.

4.3 Setting the controls

With a test pattern or exhibit on the evidence camera, the focus, color balance, and brightness and contrast controls should be set to accommodate the conditions in the courtroom.

4.3.1 Focus

Most evidence cameras have an auto-focus feature that comes on when the unit is turned on. That should be sufficient for most documents.

Manual focus is used for objects and certain kinds of exhibits that cause difficulty for the auto-focus mechanism. These are:

- Objects with low reflection factor (dark colors)
- Objects with a glossy surface (glassware, shiny plastic)
- Objects viewed through glass
- Objects with low contrast

To operate the manual focus, press the focus button and then press the N (near) or F (far) button.

4.3.2 Color balance

Most evidence cameras have an adjustment for white balance. There is usually an automatic balance feature that comes on when the unit is turned on, and this will take care of most displays.

Sometimes a large change in the ambient lighting in the courtroom (for example, if it gets darker in the afternoon and additional strong lights are turned on) will throw the white balance off. If the colors seem a little off on the screen, adjust the white balance using the controls on the front panel. Usually there is a white balance button to shift from automatic to manual mode and a knob or dial to turn from "more red" to "more blue" in adjusting so that the colors on the exhibit match the colors on the screen.

4.3.3 Brightness and contrast

An iris control on the camera adjusts brightness or exposure. If a document is dark, low contrast, or dim against a brighter background, use the exposure control to make it brighter. Turn the knob or control toward "high" to increase brightness or toward "low" to darken the image.

Sometimes the display of a very dark document or object can be improved by putting a black piece of paper behind it on the base of the evidence camera.

4.4 Zooming

In most instances, the evidence camera will be used to en-large as well as to display. Zooming is useful to focus on certain language, either a paragraph or a sentence—even words within a sentence—so that everyone is reading the same thing at the same time. Older evidence cameras require more zooming because they cannot adequately project the words of a document without enlargement

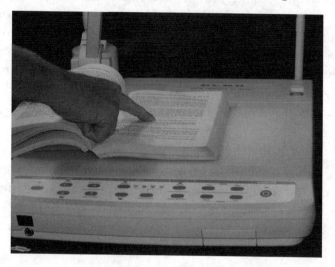

Using the evidence camera to zoom in and frame part of an exhibit is a modest exercise in eye-hand coordination using the zoom button.

- Step 1: Establish the visual anchor. Put the photo or other exhibit down on the base, and put a finger on the exhibit at a point a little below where the center of the image should be after the zoom-in is completed.

- Step 2: Press the zoom in (or "tele") button. This will start the camera zooming in.

- Step 3: Watch the monitor, not the exhibit.

- Step 4: Move the exhibit. Use the finger on the exhibit to move the exhibit so that the portion to be featured is centered under the camera. This is less difficult to do than it may sound. The finger on the exhibit is the visual anchor, and it will not be necessary to look down at the exhibit to see the move.

- Step 5: Finish the zoom. Pressing the zoom in (or "tele") button will keep the camera zooming in (focusing on a smaller and smaller area of the exhibit). Move the exhibit (gradually centering the area of interest directly under the camera) at the same time.

DO NOT zoom in randomly and then move the exhibit to get the zoom focused on the area of interest. The motion of the exhibit crossing under the camera creates a confusing visual effect and detracts from the exhibit. More importantly, the effect is likely to be disorienting to the operator and make it very difficult to get back to the portion of the exhibit that is of interest. If a mistake is made, it is better to back out a little, get oriented again, and then zoom back in.

After the testimony about an exhibit is completed and it is taken off the base, and before the next exhibit is put on the base, press the zoom out (or "wide") button to get back to where the camera started. The evidence camera is now in its "base" position, and ready to zoom in again if the next exhibit calls for that action. Zooming out can be confusing and disorienting. If the operator zooms in for one exhibit and forgets to zoom out after finishing with that exhibit, the camera will be zoomed in on some very small portion of the next exhibit put on the base. There will be no smooth flow from one exhibit to the next because the operator will need to stop and zoom out to get the current exhibit into proper focus. For this reason, some of the newer evidence cameras are equipped with presets, which take the place of holding the zoom out button to get back to the base position.

Newer equipment also has more court-friendly features such as a freeze-frame setting that allows the lawyer to move the exhibit without showing the moving frame on the monitor. This helps avoid distraction of the jury.

4.5 Reverse, flip, or rotate an image

On some models an image can be reversed (shown in a mirror image), flipped (shown upside down), or rotated 90 degrees on the screen without moving the document or object on the base of the evidence camera. If these capabilities are included, there are buttons on the front panel, buttons on the remote, and buttons on the computer display.

The reverse function is used to correct the display of reversed films or to deliberately reverse the image to change the perspective.

The flip function is used to correct the display of a document put on the base upside down.

The rotate button is used to look at an object from a different angle.

4.6 Enlarge writing on a blackboard, whiteboard, or flip chart

Occasionally a lay witness or an expert will be asked to write or mark on something that is not within easy viewing distance for the jury. The evidence camera can be used to enlarge this on a screen or monitor so all jurors can see.

Turn the camera so that the lens is pointing outward toward the board or chart instead of down toward the base of the unit.

Remove the close-up lens (if it is physically attached) or switch it off (if it is built in). This will allow the camera to focus beyond the distance from its lens to the base. Focus, adjust brightness, and zoom as necessary.

4.7 Freeze images

Some evidence cameras have a freeze frame feature that allows the operator to keep an image on the screen while the material under the camera is moved. Usually there is a freeze button that is a toggle switch—press it once to turn the freeze feature on, and press it again to turn the freeze feature off.

When finished with an exhibit, press the freeze button. Then take the exhibit off the evidence camera and put the next exhibit on the evidence camera base. When the freeze button is pressed again, the new image will appear on the screen. This avoids the eye-jarring motion that occurs when the camera follows the process of taking exhibits off the base and putting new ones on.

4.8 Capture and save images

An evidence camera can be used to scan an image of an object for use with graphics or presentation software. A laptop computer set up with a TWAIN driver can use the evidence camera as a source (like a digital camera or video camera). The image from the evidence camera is stored as a file on the computer and can be printed or inserted into a document in the same manner as any other picture.

If a witness has marked an exhibit, normally the marked exhibit will be given a separate exhibit number and handed to the court clerk. If the presenting lawyer wants to have a copy of the marked exhibit for the client's docket file, the image being displayed by the evidence camera can be saved to a laptop computer using standard presentation software or special software supplied by the manufacturer.

4.9   Integrate a PowerPoint slide show or videotape

Some evidence cameras come with special presentation software that allows the user to switch between an image generated by the evidence camera and a PowerPoint slide show resident on a laptop computer.

Some evidence cameras also have the capability to integrate video material into the evidence camera presentation. The video material can come from a tape being played by a VCR or a digital still or video camera.

Chapter 5: Exhibits for the Evidence Camera

The evidence camera works best with material that, once enlarged sufficiently, is quite clear without much additional highlighting or other marking. The camera enlarges very well, but it does not support complicated additions to an enlarged exhibit. Its best uses are photos (and similar materials such as maps and drawings), small objects, and uncomplicated material from documents.

5.1 Photos

The evidence camera is an inexpensive and flexible way to enlarge photographs, particularly those in color. Any photo can be enlarged to the desired size using the focus and zoom capabilities of the evidence camera. For example, suppose the witness testifies that a particular railroad crossing is in a commercial area. The witness has several photos of the crossing used to support this conclusion. If the cross examiner spots cows grazing in one tiny area in the upper left corner of the photo, the photo can be placed on the evidence camera base, the lawyer can zoom in until just the area featuring the cows occupies the entire display screen, and the cross-examination can proceed from there. The evidence camera produces the necessary enlargement instantly and electronically. A hard copy enlargement from the photo might take days to get and the resolution likely would not be as good.

Photos are the easiest exhibits to present using an evidence camera. Because they lie flat on the base, there are no problems with depth of field in adjusting the focus. Some photos are best presented simply by placing them on the base under the camera so that an enlarged version appears on the screen. No adjustments or other actions are required.

When a photo taken with a digital camera (or from a digital file) is printed out for use with an evidence camera, it is best printed on premium quality matte-finish (not shiny) photo paper. Shiny paper sometimes picks up glare from lighting in a courtroom. If the prints are made using a computer, the software settings must be adjusted for this kind of paper. (Click on File, select the Print option from the drop down menu. When the dialog box appears, click on the Properties button, and adjust the type of paper.)

Lawyers are accustomed to labeling photos, but standard labels sometimes do not work well with an evidence camera because the enlargement makes them too big to fit well with the underlying part of the photo. An overlay marking an area for enlargement with a small-type label on the bottom margin may work better.

Side-by-side photo comparisons can work well on an evidence camera, but sizing can be a problem with this kind of exhibit because the camera lens does not cover a wide span.

5.2 Negatives and transparencies

When the evidence camera is used to generate images of photographic negatives (including X-rays, CAT scans, and MRI images), you need to: (1) switch the backlight (located in the base) on (when the backlight is on, the upper lights will be off); (2) turn the white balance off; and (3) turn the positive/negative switch to negative.

It is important to zoom in and frame the negative to the maximum possible because the light escaping directly from the backlight will strike the camera lens and adversely affect image quality. By zooming in, this light is minimized.

X-rays, MRI images, and CAT scans

The evidence camera does an excellent job of displaying X-rays, MRI images, and CAT scans.

The evidence camera usually has a manual exposure (iris) adjustment knob, located on the camera head to get the best possible contrast for X-rays.

X-rays can be shown either in "negative" (which is their normal state) or "positive." As a negative, the X-ray displays its subject on a black background. One normally receives information on a white background, and it is easier for jurors to understand the content of the X-ray when it is displayed this way. The positive/negative switch allows you to change from negative (white on black) to positive (black on white).

35 mm slides, film negatives, and transparencies

The evidence camera will enlarge 35 mm slides to whatever size is needed. Simply put the slide on the base of the camera, turn on the base light, zoom in, and adjust the focus.

Transparencies are displayed in the same manner.

Regular negatives can be enlarged and turned into photos using the negative/positive switch. Put the negative on the base, turn the negative/positive switch to positive, and zoom in to the enlargement you need.

5.3 Small objects

Enlargement of small objects, such as computer chips or mechanical parts, allows witnesses to testify about them while showing the "real thing" on the screen.

Using the evidence camera, the object can be moved around to provide any necessary viewing angle for jury understanding of the testimony about the object. The lawyer or witness can pick up the object, rotate it on the evidence camera base so that a different side is showing, or turn it upside down. The camera will show on the screen all of these actions, so long as they are within its field of view. Relevant aspects of the object can be pointed out either by the witness standing next to the screen and indicating a location on the image or by the witness standing at the evidence camera and using a pointer directed at the object itself.

5.4 Documents

An enlarged display of words or small sections of text helps direct the jury's attention to the point to be extracted from a document. Older evidence cameras provide a limited capability to work with whole pages. A display of the entire page often reduces the text to a size too small to read. Newer cameras can display whole pages in a readable size. However, an enlarged display on the screen and the ability to interact with the document by highlighting it or pointing to a particular phrase help enhance a witness's testimony and make the evidence camera valuable in presenting simple document points.

Text document emphasis

Simple marking devices such as highlighting or under-lining can be used effectively to help focus jurors on the precise point in the document to which the lawyer is referring. Even one paragraph of text is difficult to use an as effective exhibit without a method for directing attention to the point at issue. Often the simplest mark for emphasis is the best.

Deposition transcript excerpts

Impeachment from a deposition transcript is more effective if the jurors can see the transcript at the same time the point about the inconsistency with prior testimony is being made.

It is not always easy to find the precise text on the page during the stress of cross-examination. Colored marks at the side showing the line numbers to be read can help make sure the enlargement is focused in exactly the right place.

Exhibits containing the necessary transcript excerpts can also be made ahead of time, marked in the cross-examiner's notes, and then placed on the evidence camera quickly if the testimony unfolds in a contradictory way.

Scientific, medical, or technical graphics

In many cases, the jury must learn at least some measure of scientific, medical, or technical information in order to decide the case. Often these areas are complex and the subject of extensive expert testimony. It may be useful to introduce complex information early, even in opening statement, to teach the jury enough science to understand the issues in the case.

Complicated graphics can benefit from the zoom-in capability of the evidence camera. This allows the lawyer to use published sources rather than incurring the cost of having exhibits specially prepared. However, because of the limitations of the evidence camera, care must be taken in the pace of the presentation, otherwise the jury will be left behind. Each aspect of the graphic must be taken in turn and explained slowly while the evidence camera zooms in on one part or another of the display.

Time lines

A time line shows the order in which events at issue occurred. If the passage of time, in either minutes, days, or years, or the juxtaposition of events is significant, then a time line can be an effective way to explain the meaning given by the time reference. Time lines done in hard copy are often too long, the print too small, and the data points too many. They display the time line all at once, allowing the jury to read ahead. This distracts focus from the point being made.

Time lines displayed with an evidence camera can have all of these flaws. A good time line should build entry by entry. This enables the lawyer to focus the jury on the single entry that best serves a particular point. Additional data points and expanded explanations can be added as an opening statement or witness testimony moves on. In order to do this with an evidence camera, the time line displays should be constructed in parts. The first sheet has the initial entries; the second sheet has the initial entries plus the next entry; and so on.

If the sequential entries on the time line are done as transparencies, so one sheet of the exhibit is laid directly on top of the next, it will be necessary to have a method for aligning the sheets exactly. You can tape prongs at one end of the evidence camera base and punch holes in each transparency, so that each fits over the prongs and thus is directly aligned with the sheet below.

A hard copy of the time line on a large board can be set up as a reference exhibit used to keep the main points in time within view while the evidence camera shows smaller points within the main time line events. A key aspect of constructing a good time line is to avoid too many entries. A time line needs to be clear and easy to read.

Organization charts

Informal organization charts that show who reports to whom, or who is responsible for supervising whom, can be helpful in avoiding confusion when the evidence includes quite a few names. It is not necessary for the company or organization to have an official chart so long as the exhibit accurately reflects qualified testimony.

Statistical charts

Statistical charts can be confusing if presented all at once. These displays need to "build" so, for example, the bars on a bar chart or the slices of a pie chart appear one at a time as the lawyer explains the significance of what is being shown. By explaining each segment separately, the lawyer makes it easier for jurors to understand the whole.

5.5 Books and newspapers

The evidence camera allows you to show the entire book that your witness is using to bolster testimony, then turn to the section of the book in which the material you intend to emphasize is located, and finally to arrive at the page on which the material appears. The jury can follow this easily with the enlarged images on the screen.

Narrow columns of text

The evidence camera works well with narrow column text. The focus of many older cameras is limited to a span about 5 inches wide. Columns of about 2 inches, such as newspaper format, can be enlarged readily.

The columns of condensed print on minuscript transcripts also work well on the evidence camera. Put the page down on the base under the camera. Use the zoom in feature to get to the particular text in which you are interested. You can now have the witness use the text working directly from the image on the screen while you point to it with your finger or pen.

5.6 Bullet point lists

Simple bullet point slides that outline the opening statement provide a very effective way for new users of courtroom technology to stay focused and get away from notes on a yellow pad. Bullet points work best with a laptop computer setup (see chapter 10), but can be adapted for the evidence camera.

The most basic rule about bullet points is that they should come up one at a time so that the audience cannot read ahead. With an evidence camera, this can be done either with a cover (a piece of paper that slides down to reveal the points one-by-one) or by successive pages, each containing one additional point.

Opening statements guided by bullet points are often shorter and more to the point. Inexperienced lawyers sometimes fear objections if they use these displays during an opening statement. However, the general rule governing bullet point displays is that the words on the display are not objectionable if they could be spoken by the lawyer without objection during the opening statement.

Chapter 6: Making Presentations with the Evidence Camera

The evidence camera's simple operation and observable connection between object and display on the screen make it a good choice for personal operation by the trial lawyer. When the lawyer picks up a document and puts it down on the evidence camera base, the enlarged image of the document appears immediately on the screen. Jurors see exactly how the operation works. When a lawyer says, "Directing your attention to the portion of this photograph above the first floor of the house," and puts the photo on the evidence camera base and presses the zoom button to bring an enlarged image of this area to the screen, the natural flow between the lawyer's words and the screen display enhances the appearance of competence and control.

The principal techniques for making the evidence presentation more effective with an evidence camera are set out below.

6.1 Enlarging

Zooming in is a natural action that is easily followed visually. The best technique for most exhibits is to show the whole exhibit, zoom in to show a section of the exhibit and finish the point with the witness while the evidence camera remains zoomed in. In that way, the jury sees the exhibit as a whole and understands the context of the part that is being explained.

For example, a lawyer might have an aerial photo of a city block and want to show the group of buildings that were damaged when the city's water main broke. She would start with the hard copy of the photo and have the witness identify it. Next, she would put the hard copy on the evidence camera and have the witness identify it again, preferably with its exhibit number showing. She would then ask the witness to point to the area where buildings were affected by the flood and to identify the cross streets. Finally, she would zoom in on that point until the camera frames only the buildings about which the witness will testify.

In nearly every case, the user will zoom *in* while the jury is watching and zoom *out* while nothing is being displayed and therefore the jury is not watching.

In a few instances, one might want to start with the evidence camera zoomed in and then zoom out to a broader view. For example, if the purpose is to show a family relationship, a lawyer or witness might start with the evidence camera zoomed in on an inset photo of the individual and then zoom out to show that individual's place in the family group or family tree. In a loss of consortium case, one might start zoomed in on the child alone and then zoom back to an extended family.

Zoom out can also be used to deal with photos that are out of context. Suppose that opposing counsel has a photo tightly focused on subject matter favorable to his case. Examining counsel needs to show that, in a wider context, the photo would show details favorable to her case. She could start in a zoomed in position with the photo, then put behind the photo a piece of paper containing a drawing or illustration of the missing details and zoom out to show the broader context.

§6.1

Zoom out can also occasionally be used with documents. If opposing counsel has focused on one or two words in the fine print, it may be useful to take the jury from those words back to the mass of fine print that faced the person who agreed to the insurance contract.

When presenting an object, it is useful for the jury to see the object in "real life size" first, perhaps accompanied by an introductory explanation from the witness before the object is put on the evidence camera. If the "real thing" is totally unfamiliar to the average juror, and it is important to the case, use a large board with a blowup of a photo or a diagram before introducing the "real thing." After these initial steps, go to the evidence camera and zoom in for the explanation of the details.

6.2 Anchoring

Normally it is not important for jurors to focus on an entire page of a document because their attention will be directed to just a small portion of the page. When the page is put on the evidence camera base, counsel should focus initially (for at least five seconds) on something that reassures the jurors that this page is what it is supposed to be, such as the exhibit number, the title, a page number, or some other anchoring mark. Counsel should then move immediately to the words, sentences, or other portion on which the jurors should focus. Zoom right up against the edges of the margins of the text to eliminate all the white space around the edges of the document. This maneuver may take some practice before being able to get to the margins directly without eye-wobbling zooms in and out.

Occasionally, a persuasive point will be enhanced by focusing first on a word or phrase on a page and then zooming out to the full page in order to show that word in context. This technique should be used very sparingly as jurors have a difficult time focusing on a zoom out and may not be able to follow the point at all.

6.3 Pointing

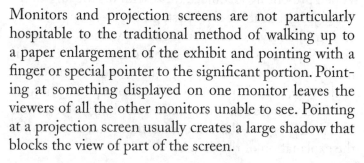

Monitors and projection screens are not particularly hospitable to the traditional method of walking up to a paper enlargement of the exhibit and pointing with a finger or special pointer to the significant portion. Pointing at something displayed on one monitor leaves the viewers of all the other monitors unable to see. Pointing at a projection screen usually creates a large shadow that blocks the view of part of the screen.

Pointing needs to be done at the evidence camera itself, rather than at the display device. Use a pencil, pen tip, or special-purpose stick pointer to direct the viewer's attention to something on the exhibit. If a considerable amount of pointing will be required during the course of the trial, one alternative is the use of annotation equipment that can be cabled to the evidence camera setup to superimpose marks or drawing on any image generated by the evidence camera. See explanation in section 10.2.2.

Some practitioners like to point with a finger. However, the enlarged image of the fingertip may obliterate the view of the object, and viewers may concentrate on the display of the fingernail rather than the exhibit.

The remote control for the evidence camera may have a pointing device—usually an arrow, sometimes a red dot that appears on the screen, occasionally an icon with a pointing finger. None of these work well. The remote tends to wobble and it is difficult for viewers to focus on the very small indicator on the screen.

6.4 Highlighting

A standard yellow highlighter can be used to draw attention to the precise text to which the witness's attention is being directed. Other colors are available to make related or contrasting points, but yellow is generally most effective for highlighting.

It is usually a good practice to premark the exhibit with the highlighting to be used. Occasionally the lawyer may want to mark the text as the witness proceeds, however this technique should be reserved for unusual occasions where this method of emphasis is needed because the lawyer is responding to an unexpected point. The action of highlighting distracts the jury's attention from the substance of what is being said.

A photo can be highlighted by marking directly on the surface with a colored marker. An easier technique is to put the photo in a plastic sleeve and use a grease pencil to mark on the plastic. This way, the sleeve can be marked as a separate exhibit if necessary, and the original photo escapes unscathed. Use a sleeve with a matte finish, not a shiny finish, to avoid glare on the evidence camera base.

6.5 Sizing

When a small object is put on the base of the evidence camera, put a normal ruler next to the object. When the zoom is used to enlarge the object, the tick marks on the ruler will also enlarge and keep the size of the object in perspective.

6.6 Covers

One way to get the jury to follow text line-by-line is to put a blank piece of paper on top of the text document and pull it down the page one line or one paragraph at a time. The blank piece of paper is a "cover."

Sometimes there is a need to highlight text by blocking out other, irrelevant, text. This can be done by putting a cover, usually a blank piece of paper, over the portions to be blanked out. This technique often works better than displaying a prepared exhibit with the irrelevant sections already removed because the jury can see that the material has not really been removed, just covered up to assist their focus. Jurors may assume that lawyers have done something sneaky when redacted documents appear on the screen. The evidence camera gets around this problem.

6.7 Background

A light-colored or white object on the base or the evidence camera may not produce a good image on the screen. Documents printed on white paper do not show up well on the screen without a background.

For documents, put a piece of black construction paper or a piece of black rubber over the white rectangle on the base of the evidence camera. This will make the document stand out better and appear with a more realistic, "document-like" image on the screen.

For light-colored or white objects, use a piece of colored paper on the base and set the white object on top of it to create the necessary contrast. Blue or green paper is usually a good background. Light colors, and particularly yellow, do not work well as a background because they mislead the iris on the camera. The auto-iris decreases the amount of light to compensate for the light background and the image gets darker. Darker colors like dark brown or black also may cause problems because they absorb light. Try out the color scheme to be used in order to ensure that the resulting image is clear and sharp.

Chapter 7: Pretrial Preparations

This chapter covers aspects of the pretrial process that may affect the successful use of an evidence camera in the courtroom.

7.1 Acceptance by the court

Although evidence cameras have been in use in courtrooms for about fifteen years, there are still many judges out there who have never presided over a trial at which this kind of equipment has been used. These judges are sometimes resistant to new techniques. Alternatively, a judge may work in a courtroom that is equipped with an evidence camera and, although the court-supplied equipment is old and not very capable, the judge may resist allowing the lawyer to bring in newer, better equipment.

When a courtroom does not have its own equipment, several key considerations affect the practicality of what lawyers may propose.

Precedent

A judge who has never had particular equipment operating in his or her courtroom may have a negative reaction when faced with a request to use it for a trial. The best precedent is successful operation in another courtroom in the same jurisdiction, or a nearby jurisdiction. Whatever the lawyers want to bring into the courtroom should not unduly disturb the appearance of the courtroom as a dignified place where serious matters are considered. The court may not be able to make a decision about this factor without seeing the actual equipment in the courtroom as the lawyers propose to set it up, or consulting with another judge who has presided at a trial in which the equipment was used. If a previous trial using tech equipment has been held in the courtroom, it is useful to inquire how that went.

Physical space

The available space in the courtroom may foreclose certain options. For example, a projection screen normally needs to be at least 10 feet from the jury box and placed where all jurors have an almost straight-on viewing angle. If the courtroom does not have the requisite space, then this alternative is not available and large monitors at either end of the jury box might be considered.

Positioning

Even if the use of proposed equipment is acceptable to the court, and the physical space will accommodate the equipment, the positioning of the equipment in the courtroom may be disadvantageous to the other party. For example, the images appearing on large monitors that face the jury box head on will not be visible from the far counsel table although they may be readily visible to the counsel table nearest the jury box. The positioning of equipment may also be disadvantageous to the jury. For example, a projection screen that is set up far away from the witness box may make it harder for the jury to focus on information delivered by an expert witness.

The court, counsel, witnesses, and jury all should have unobstructed sight lines. Sometimes it is possible to persuade the court to come down from the bench to view the displays so that the equipment can be positioned successfully for the jury, the witness, and opposing counsel. It is useful to get these issues worked out well before trial. A brief pretrial session may be required in which the parties appear with the equipment they intend to use, hook it up in a temporary fashion, and display either real or test exhibits so the court or the courtroom deputy can see how it is intended to operate.

Lighting

Strong natural daylight coming through windows facing a monitor may make large monitors impractical because they will be too hard to see. Small individual monitors in the jury box may be the only practical alternative.

Overhead lighting directly above a projection screen will wash out the image on the screen. (Sunlight coming through windows facing the screen will have the same effect.) If that lighting cannot be turned off selectively by loosening a few bulbs (while maintaining the rest of the lighting in the courtroom) or blocked by taping cardboard temporarily over the fixtures, the large screen may not work. Turning off all the lights in the courtroom is generally a bad idea as people doze in the dark, and witnesses cannot be observed to determine credibility.

Infrastructure

The nature and quality of the electrical outlets in the courtroom may be a limiting factor. The outlets cannot be overloaded or fuses will be blown. Evidence cameras, monitors, and projectors have independent power cords that need to be plugged into an outlet. Power strips can provide additional connections so long as the circuits are adequate.

Cabling

The amount of special cabling required for a proposed installation may lead the court to consider alternatives. For example, the cabling necessary for a temporary installation of small monitors in the jury box may be too much for the practical use of the jury box day in and day out.

Safety

All of the equipment brought into the courtroom needs solid support on a table or stand so that it does not tip over on someone or cause disruption. The cabling and electrical power cords need to be taped to the floor to ensure no one trips and falls.

7.2 Disclosure

Most knowledgeable lawyers will press for pretrial disclosure with respect to the equipment to be used at trial by an opponent. Most experienced judges will require disclosure because it helps prevent trial-by-ambush and allows rational planning so that the case can be tried expeditiously. It is very difficult to deal with technology disputes on the morning of trial when one side starts lugging large boxes of equipment into the courtroom or during trial when one side starts to lay the foundation for an unexpected exhibit.

Disclosure as to equipment

The usual requirement for disclosure as to equipment to be used in the courtroom is about the same as disclosure required with respect to witnesses—enough information to allow opposing counsel and the court to understand what is going to be used.

Each side will normally list the equipment supplied by the court that it may use. This process helps highlight potential technical demands on the court staff. For example, if the court has videoconference equipment and one side plans to use it, the court staff that sets up the videoconference can be alerted.

Each side also usually lists separately the equipment, if any, that it plans to bring into the courtroom. The list of imported equipment should include all the supporting switches, converters, cabling, and controls that will be used. This will highlight potential operational problems. Disclosure of equipment to be brought in also helps spot duplication of the kind that can be eliminated (e.g., monitors) thus reducing clutter in the courtroom, and allows sharing to be considered. Disclosure does not solve all problems of surprise. One lawyer may still sandbag another by listing no equipment to be brought in, and then asking to use the opponent's equipment just before beginning a cross-examination.

Disclosure as to exhibits

Many courts will consider requiring disclosure with respect to everything that will be shown to the jury. The timing of disclosure may be different with respect to evidentiary exhibits, expert materials, and illustrative aids.

Normally all prospective evidentiary exhibits in civil cases are disclosed relatively early and listed during pretrial preparation under the court's standard pretrial order. In civil cases, most visual displays used by an expert are treated as part of the expert's report for disclosure purposes, and pretrial orders may contain explicit provisions in this regard that are more detailed than the rules. On the other hand, simple bullet point lists of items covered in the expert's report, for example the materials reviewed by the expert, are often not constructed until shortly before trial and usually would not prejudice the other side if disclosed before the expert's testimony.

Illustrative aids, other than those used with experts, present a more diverse problem with respect to disclosure. Knowledgeable lawyers usually request (and give) disclosure of illustrative aids in the form and format that will be used at trial. In other words, the exchange should provide the materials in a way that allows the opponent to see what is coming. For example, disclosure via black and white paper copies of exhibits does not disclose any color that may be involved in the exhibit.

7.3 Shared use of equipment

Most equipment brought into the courtroom involves matters within the court's discretion. The basic argument for sharing equipment applies regardless of whether one lawyer or the other requests it and, for that reason, the court may raise it sua sponte. If the court permits one party to bring equipment into the courtroom, the other party should not be denied the same opportunity to have access to these means of displaying exhibits. However, having two evidence cameras, two sets of monitors, or two projection screens is usually disadvantageous to the court because of the clutter and waste of time that may occur.

The matter may also come up in a contested way—one party will ask that any equipment being brought into the courtroom be available to both sides, and the other party will refuse. Some lawyers refuse as a reflex action. If they are not familiar with the equipment, they may not appreciate circumstances under which there is no work product involved or they may believe the court has no basis to order sharing.

In considering sharing, it is useful to separate equipment into three categories:

- **Display devices.** Equipment to display exhibits includes evidence cameras, projectors, projection screens, monitors, annotation tools, converters, switches, controls, and cabling. This equipment can be shared because it contains no work product and is unlikely to sustain any damage. Sharing promotes efficiency and good order in the courtroom by avoiding dueling sets of the same equipment.

- **Laptop computers.** The laptop typically contains files and software used to retrieve exhibits and transmit them to the monitor or projector, to receive input from real time reporting, and to communicate back to the office. Generally, laptops are not shared because they contain work product and may crash if misused.

- **Equipment brought in by an expert witness.** Experts occasionally bring equipment to the courtroom for purposes of demonstrating some aspect of their testimony. Equipment brought in by experts needs to be considered on a case-by-case basis. If it is more like a laptop, and contains identifiable work product or requires special expertise to operate, perhaps it should not be shared. If it is more like the normal display equipment, containing no work product and requiring no special expertise to operate, normally it should be shared.

Cost-sharing may be important if the equipment is not already available in the courtroom. There are commercial rental rates for all of the equipment used in courtroom presentations, so it is relatively easy to determine fair shares.

An additional consideration is whether to request the use of "better" equipment in order to save time and provide the best displays for the jury. For example, the digital projector selected by one side may be adequate for displaying one kind of exhibit but the other side may want to use a better projector to display different kinds of exhibits. This occurs primarily when the projector has a rating below 1,000 lumens and the exhibits contain a lot of text. Projectors with lower ratings work relatively well with brightly colored photos, but they do not produce as distinct an image of dense text documents, and they may produce quite a bit of distracting noise from the fan that cools the unit.

Shared use of equipment operators

The question of shared access to an equipment operator may come up when one side is well equipped and the other is not. Shared use may put the operator in a difficult position. Operators and technicians often work with the trial lawyers outside the courtroom and may know information that is privileged or confidential. Operators may "practice" with the lead lawyer or the expert witness for the party that retained them. Requiring them to work with opponents other than in merely ministerial ways (plugging in the equipment, finding a spare bulb) usually makes these nonlawyers very uncomfortable.

For example, one side may bring in an evidence camera, a projector, and a large projection screen so that photographs and other exhibits can be shown to the jury in enlarged format. If there are a large number of exhibits, the lead lawyer may have a technician or paralegal handle the evidence camera during trial. Now the other side wants to use both the evidence camera and the technician. One of the other side's exhibits is put on the evidence camera. The technician knows that this exhibit would look better if the zoom function were used to focus on the area of the exhibit about which the witness is currently testifying, but the opposing lawyer has not requested this. The technician is pulled between helping the other side to perform better and loyalty to the trial lawyer for whom he or she works. If an operator is necessary, a better option may be to have the opposing lawyer provide a paralegal who can spend the short time necessary to learn how to operate the evidence camera.

7.4 Practice with the equipment

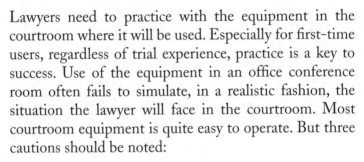

Lawyers need to practice with the equipment in the courtroom where it will be used. Especially for first-time users, regardless of trial experience, practice is a key to success. Use of the equipment in an office conference room often fails to simulate, in a realistic fashion, the situation the lawyer will face in the courtroom. Most courtroom equipment is quite easy to operate. But three cautions should be noted:

- **Different controls.** The controls are not always immediately intuitive. In particular, the control panels (if any) in the courtroom used to integrate the court's equipment may be different from the controls used elsewhere. Witnesses may be frustrated with the equipment unless they have had a chance to try it out ahead of time.

- **Different effects.** The effect of particular displays on small monitors or a large projection screen in the courtroom space may be quite different from the image on an 8 x 10-inch hard copy. A visual display that looks just fine in hard copy may look washed out and quite illegible on the large screen in the courtroom. Projectors treat colors differently than monitors do, with variations among projectors as well, and a particular projector's settings may make red look like a darker color, or turn green slightly yellow. Digital projectors have a menu button that brings up controls to vary the brightness and coloration. Doing a test in the courtroom ahead of time to check on the reds and greens, for example, is a must.

§7.4

Chapter 8: Trial

This chapter covers the use of the evidence camera at trial including impacts on preliminary matters, jury selection, preliminary jury instructions, opening statements, working with witnesses, and closing arguments. The discussion in this part is set against the backdrop of the Federal Rules of Evidence. A generalized discussion, without reference to a specific set of evidentiary rules, is less useful when the focus moves to trials. In the matters that affect the use of courtroom technology, the Federal Rules reflect the practices in the majority of states although each state has its own peculiarities.

8.1 Preliminary matters

At the beginning of a trial using courtroom technology, representations from counsel, review of backup arrangements, identification of equipment operators, and testing the kill switch that allows the judge to blank all visuals shown to the jury are useful for the appellate record and for saving time later in trial. Even a trial that is expected to last only a few days usually benefits from the ten minutes spent on the standard set of preliminary matters geared to the technology to be used.

Representations about equipment and testing

Representations from counsel at the outset of trial are a useful way to create a record as to the equipment that might be used during trial and a way to deal with some potential appellate issues arising out of its use. This is not a substitute for disclosure, discussed in chapter 7, but the creation of the necessary record about what is taking place in the courtroom. It takes less than five minutes to get the standard representations on the record.

Equipment. Each party should describe the equipment that they will be using. This may be the court's equipment or supplemental devices brought to the courtroom especially for trial. A typical representation with respect to an evidence camera might go something like this: "Your Honor, we have an evidence camera that will assist in displaying some of the exhibits we will be using. The output of the evidence camera will be displayed through a projector on a large screen here in the courtroom." Once this representation is completed, the court can inquire of the opposing party if they have any objection to the use of the equipment as described.

Inspection. Each party should state that they have had an opportunity to inspect any projection or display equipment present in the courtroom. This includes the monitors, screens, projectors, printers, evidence cameras, cables, switches, wiring, and the like brought into the courtroom by an opponent—probably everything except the contents of the opposing lawyer's personal laptop computer. There are no legitimate work product issues with projection and display equipment.

Testing. If the court supplies equipment, a party who uses that equipment should represent that it has had an opportunity to test the equipment and that it works satisfactorily. Most difficulties with evidence camera equipment can be spotted with a simple pretrial check. This will avoid the inevitable request for a break if the equipment fails to work the first time someone tries to use it during the trial. If a party plans to bring equipment to the courtroom, to use either standing alone or in conjunction with the court's equipment, it is useful to have a representation about compatibility and reliability. Projectors, evidence cameras, laptops, and monitors all have little quirks that may prevent them from working together on the first try. Just because they worked fine in the lawyer's office is no guarantee that they will work fine in the courtroom.

Positioning of equipment. If one side or the other has brought equipment to the courtroom, each side should represent that they are satisfied with the positioning of the equipment in the courtroom. This obviates later arguments that a line of sight to the court, jury, or an exhibit is blocked in which case the court may have to consider a request that the equipment be moved.

Kill switch. If monitors are used to display the output of an evidence camera, there normally will be a kill switch that takes an image off all the monitors within the view of jurors. This can be tested by having counsel put an image on the screen and pressing the switch. It is useful to have a test graphic for this purpose that has nothing to do with the case. If equipment has been brought to the courtroom, either to supplement the court's equipment or to stand alone, it is important to establish at the outset that the images projected anywhere a juror can see them can be controlled by the kill switch. Judges who work in courtrooms with small monitors in the jury box usually have a court-installed kill switch at the bench. Lawyers need to be sure the jurors' monitors have been turned back on if the kill switch is used by the court during trial. The lawyers will not know that the jurors' monitors are still off because the images will be showing on their monitors (which would not have been turned off). This usually comes to light only when a lawyer refers to something that should be appearing on the screen, and the jurors are all looking up wondering what is happening.

Identification of operators

Each party should identify anyone who will be operating the party's equipment in the courtroom. These equipment operators may need to be in the well of the court, and it is useful to know who they are.

Backup in case of equipment failure

Lawyers should focus on what will happen if the equipment fails. Normal backup arrangements are straight forward:

Evidence camera. Backup is usually either (1) a backup evidence camera unit, (2) acetate transparencies on an overhead projector, or (3) paper copies of exhibits that can be handed to the jurors.

Projector. The most likely failure on a projector is a burned out bulb, so having a spare backup bulb is prudent. Projector bulbs now have an extended lifetime of around 1,000 hours. The menu button on the projector will display a screen (after going through the various options) showing the number of hours used or the number of hours left on the bulb.

If the projector goes out for some other reason, and the courtroom has monitors, the evidence camera can be cabled to the monitors.

Alternatively, because the evidence camera cannot display anything without either a projector or monitors, the backup would revert to the backup for the evidence camera itself (see above).

Projection screen. In a front projection system, the projection screen is a simple mechanical device and almost nothing can go wrong with it.

Monitors. Rental monitors are usually available immediately from local audio-visual suppliers as replacements for monitors that fail during courtroom use.

Equipment failures are not usually a problem once the equipment is running. One judge reports that in four years of using electronic equipment for most trials, he has had only one total collapse of the equipment. Almost all failures occur on the first day the equipment is used, generally because someone failed to connect cabling properly. However, as one court has pointed out in its guidance on the use of presentation technology, Murphy was an optimist.

8.2 Jury selection

Use of projection and display equipment in the courtroom raises a few additional matters to be addressed during jury selection. Questions that would seem unusual in the traditional context are, in fact, necessary to determine how technology-driven exhibits must be created or changed to accommodate the needs of jurors.

Visual acuity

Visual displays on large monitors outside the jury box or on projection screens require that jurors have the capability to read at a distance. Some people who cannot see well wear glasses for close-up reading but do not get the bifocals or second set of glasses that they would need to read at a distance. They find that their distance vision is good enough for most things, and they are not concerned about reading at a distance because they are rarely called upon to do that.

When these people arrive for jury duty, they may have their regular glasses, but when a visual display shows up on a monitor or screen some distance away, they cannot read it. This is a serious problem in a trial in which the parties rely on visual displays to help make key points. For that reason, it is usually a good idea to put something up on the screen that will be used for exhibits and inquire whether anyone has any difficulty reading it. Alternatively the lawyer who uses visual displays might ask the court to ask jurors who wear glasses for any purpose whether they have prescriptions to correct distance vision. If they do, they can be asked to bring that set of glasses when they come to court the next day and can be told why this is necessary. These inquiries may seem less intrusive if made by the court.

Small monitors inside the jury box can be seen very well with ordinary correction for close-up vision and generally are less problematic because people tend to carry with them any glasses needed for close-up reading. Nevertheless, it may be useful to remind farsighted jurors to bring their reading glasses to court.

Color blindness

Some significant portion of the population, perhaps one person in five, is color-blind. Scientists seem to disagree about the exact percentage, but because of the hereditary nature of color blindness, it afflicts a larger number of males than females. Genetic color-blindness generally does not involve a complete inability to see colors. It is usually an inability to distinguish reds and greens and differentiate small tonal variations of other colors. Color-blindness resulting from age usually occurs after about age fifty and is typically an inability to discern variations of blue.

Some kinds of visual displays that depend on color to make a point can be misleading to color-blind jurors. These people will have trouble, for example, with a bar chart that uses red and green to compare amounts, or a pie chart that uses shades of blue to differentiate shares of some given amount. Other aspects of visual displays may also be perceived differently to color-blind jurors than to other jurors. Deliberations may be difficult if jurors saw different things.

It is useful to inquire, as a routine item during jury selection, whether anyone is color-blind. Most people who are color-blind know about their condition because it affects many small aspects of everyday life. This information provides an opportunity to adjust the colors on exhibits or to make sure that oral explanations take account of the fact that some jurors cannot see certain color differences on the screen.

Tolerance for television

Jury science consultants advise lawyers that the amount of television watched by a prospective juror affects how quickly he or she is ready to absorb the content of a visual display and move on. People who watch a lot of television, consultants find, feel comfortable with a pace that is considerably faster than people who get most of their information or entertainment by reading newspapers and books or listening to radio. In making presentations, lawyers often regard it as important to know if there are "paper-oriented" people on the jury so that the timing of the displays can be adjusted. Readers get impatient and annoyed if they are not allowed enough time to examine all aspects of a display thoroughly, and it disappears before they are finished considering it. Watchers are accustomed to looking at displays in a more general way and assume that if they didn't get the message the first time, more will be coming.

8.3 Preliminary jury instructions

The use of an evidence camera raises the question whether the court should include in the preliminary instructions a brief introduction or orientation to the equipment.

For the same reason that courts have traditionally introduced court personnel—the clerks, bailiffs, and reporters—it is helpful for the court to provide a short orientation to the equipment in the courtroom. Most jurors are very comfortable with the equipment, and do not need a lot of information about how it is going to work. However, a brief introduction ensures that all jurors are informed. If the court does an introduction, the lawyers do not have to introduce the equipment during opening statement, and the court's statement makes clear that the equipment (even if brought in by one side) is a part of the court's regular proceedings and does not favor one side or the other.

It is useful for lawyers to inquire of the court at some appropriate point whether any orientation as to the courtroom's equipment will be included in the court's preliminary instructions. If the court does not do any orientation in this regard, the same kind of statements can be used by lawyers in an opening statement. A standard set of statements about equipment (that would be amended depending on what is in the courtroom) is set out below.

Monitors. "Our courtroom is wired so that the lawyers can display on monitors the documents or photographs or other things that are involved in the case. I have a monitor here at the bench. Each lawyer has a monitor. There is a monitor for the witness." [Add a sentence on juror monitors if they are used. If the monitors for the jury are outside the jury box, ask if everyone can see the monitor. If the monitors for the jury are inside the jury box, describe the extent to which jurors can control the brightness or contrast on their monitors.]

Evidence camera. "We have an evidence camera next to the lectern. It is the device with the small box on top of an arm, and two lights on arms above its base. The evidence camera is a stationary video camera. It works like any other video camera. If you put something in front of its lens, it transmits a picture. In this case, the video camera is hooked up to display its pictures on the monitors in the courtroom."

Projector and projection screen. "We have a projector located over there. That projector is cabled to receive input from the evidence camera. It displays enlarged pictures of what it receives on the projection screen over there."

Kill switch. "I have a control switch, or cutoff switch, here on the bench. This permits me to control the presentation of evidence to you so that if there is an objection, I can press the cutoff switch and your screens will go blank while I discuss with the lawyers whether the item is appropriate for viewing. That is normal and standard procedure, and you should not draw any inference one way or the other when I use the cutoff switch."

These explanations help jurors who may have less familiarity with the technology and might feel at a disadvantage in discussions with jurors who have a good deal of knowledge about electronics or computer equipment. It also helps avoid speculation among the jurors about the equipment by making it all just a part of the courtroom environment.

The practice of allowing evidentiary exhibits to go to the jury room but withholding illustrative aids is a mystery to most jurors. For this reason, it is useful to explain how this works at the outset in the preliminary instructions if the case is likely to involve a substantial number of illustrative aids. For example:

> Because this courtroom is equipped as I have described, the lawyers may use illustrative aids in their opening statements and at other times during trial to assist you in understanding the evidence. However, illustrative aids are not evidence. They are presented so that you can focus more efficiently on the evidence during the trial. They are very similar to the verbal comments of lawyers in opening statements and closing arguments: comments that are not evidence but which should be helpful to you in understanding the evidence. Just like the verbal comments of lawyers, you will not have the illustrative aids in the jury room when you retire to deliberate. At that time, you will consider only sworn testimony of the witnesses and the exhibits that have been admitted into evidence.

In jurisdictions where juror note taking is permitted, the court might consider adding: "If you find that an illustrative aid is helpful to you in understanding or organizing the evidence, you are allowed, but not required, to describe it in your personal notes."

8.4 Opening statements

Opening statements are the most likely part of the trial for electronic displays to appear. Most litigation consultants urge lawyers to include graphics in their opening statements. Trial practice courses deliver the same message. And lawyers are quick to see the advantages in making opening statements more interesting, compelling, and expeditious. For these reasons, even if there are very few uses of courtroom technology in other parts of the case, some visuals may be used during opening statement.

The more technology to be used in the trial, the more the beginning of the opening statement should be kept low tech and personal. Jurors will only accept what is presented on a screen or monitor if they accept the lawyer as a credible, understandable person who is delivering the display. An evidence camera is very low tech and can be made quite personal if the lawyer delivering the opening operates the equipment directly. It is particularly effective against an opponent who uses PowerPoint slides a great deal. The evidence camera shows the "real thing" (e.g., an enlargement of a photo, a good view of a small object, a portion of text from a document) and contrasts well against bullet point summaries.

As noted in section 8.3, if the court declines to include in the preliminary jury instructions an explanation of the equipment that will be used during trial, the opening statement should introduce the technology and any operator who will be assisting in its use. Do this after establishing what the case is about. Never lead with equipment. The opening should cover each item of equipment and inform the jury briefly how it will be used in presenting the client's case. Using the equipment to display visuals that are a part of the opening is a good platform for this explanation. Reassure jurors that they will have hard copy of every exhibit when they go to the jury room, and tell them that the equipment is primarily for the purpose of saving time.

Some courts routinely require counsel to show each other what will be used in opening at a set time (perhaps several days) before trial and to submit any objections. However, lawyers may be tinkering with their opening statements at the last moment and the "final" versions of the supporting slides may not be created until shortly before they are used. It is often administratively easier (and serves the purpose of checking out the equipment as well) to just run quickly through the illustrative aids for opening statement as a preliminary matter at trial.

Knowledgeable counsel will almost always request that the court review all graphics displays to be used in opening statement. The most frequent exception occurs when counsel is planning to sandbag an unsuspecting opponent with graphics that might draw an objection if a less-prepared opponent has time to think about the basis for an objection.

8.5 Working with witnesses

The evidence camera is a supporting prop, not the star of the show. Except for witnesses called only to authenticate exhibits, the camera should make very limited appearance until the witness has firmly established credibility through presentation of material.

Individual witnesses relate to an evidence camera differently. Some are most effective if they concentrate on testifying, while the lawyer controls the display and points to the items the witness is explaining. Others are at their best when they come down off the stand, walk to the evidence camera, and put on their own displays pointing to significant items so that the pointer appears with the image on the screen. If annotation equipment is available (see section 10.2.2), the witness can mark on the display with an electronic overlay to illustrate key features or points.

The witness as an operator is a very effective way to present evidence, and some courtrooms are equipped with evidence cameras at the witness stand for this purpose.

When the person with the information (not the lawyer advocate) is at the controls, jurors may be significantly more receptive and interested. However, controlling the display while talking in the high-stress environment of a courtroom is more than some witnesses can handle.

The evidence camera is also very useful for cross-examination. It provides a flexible way to display any paper exhibit quickly and effectively. When the witness is being asked to re-examine a document, the jury can easily follow along if the lawyer is pointing to or marking up the contested language on the screen.

A display on the evidence camera can be used in cross by writing on a document with handmade callouts of important facts, or in a side-by-side presentation underlining differences. The evidence camera can also be used the way the old-fashioned flip chart was used—as a place to write down what was said on direct, quotes from various sources as part of an impeachment, or to make a list of points about which the witness was wrong. All of this can be done right in front of the jury, in real time so to speak, with a display that is large enough for everyone in the courtroom to see. Particularly in a trial dominated by technology displays, this kind of use of the evidence camera is very down-to-earth and effective.

8.6 Closing argument

Closing argument can be made much shorter and better with the use of good illustrative aids. Lawyers tend to stay on point when guided by an organized presentation of the evidence and arguments. Fewer illustrative aids are objectionable in the context of a closing. The general rule is that if the lawyer could make a statement or comment orally, or could write it on a blackboard in the traditional manner, without objection, then there should be no sustainable objection to an illustrative aid that does the same thing.

Knowledgeable lawyers usually ask for disclosure of a few kinds of displays in advance of closing arguments in order to protect against potential inappropriate uses.

New material. Photographic or graphics materials that have not been marked as exhibits in the case are at the head of the list of things that might usefully be disclosed so that the court can consider objections before closing argument starts. Lawyers occasionally get carried away with the possibilities for analogies. The bound volume of a Bible sometimes makes a cameo appearance in closing; a photo of the *Titanic* sinking has been a favorite in the past; and images from advertisements are occasionally used to make a rhetorical point. All of these are objectionable.

Other dangers of irretrievable prejudicial effect on the jury come from video, photo, or graphics materials. An example in this category (that can go either way) is using photos of witnesses that are single frames picked off deposition videos in order to remind the jury, in closing argument, about the witness testimony. Many jurors have more personal reactions to witnesses they liked and did not like when reminded by a photo.

New color. Exhibits in the case to which color has been added for purposes of closing argument should also be reviewed in advance. Occasionally superimposing one exhibit on another falls into this category, although if both images are in evidence, superimposing one over the other would not usually be a problem. The principal danger, indeed often the objective, is that jurors will confuse the closing argument display with the real exhibit. This technique may be the only practical way for one side to tackle the other side's most persuasive exhibit, but the opposing counsel may be entitled to see the proposed visual display in advance.

New digitally altered photos. Although no digitally altered photos may have been used at trial, occasionally a point on closing argument can be made effectively by altering a photo that is in evidence to illustrate the point. Lawyers may want to change the photo to illustrate the persuasive nature of their own argument or the gaps in logic in their opponent's argument. If it is not made very clear to the jury that the photo has been changed, there may be confusion in the jurors' minds about the exhibits.

Testimony from the transcript. It may be useful to a lawyer to invite close jury scrutiny of the testimony of a particular witness. One technique for doing this is to use portions of the transcript, enlarged on the projection screen or monitors, with underlining and labels as to page and line numbers. Using the evidence camera for emphasizing parts of a transcript in ways that could have been done by the lawyer orally or by hand-drawn emphasis on a paper exhibit introduces no new bases for objection. This is usually a suggestion to the jurors that they ask for the transcript and study it themselves, but is not objectionable on that ground alone. However, the manner of emphasis of particular words in the testimony may be objectionable if not accurately reflective of the testimony. For example, using a full page of the transcript and drawing lines under words used by the witness is not objectionable. Writing words from the transcript in its margin and drawing fair inferences is not objectionable. However, pulling out individual words and assembling them so as to suggest content not in the testimony is manipulative and unduly predjudicial, and this becomes objectionable.

Even though counsel are now presenting arguments, and the narrower rules governing opening statements no longer apply, some displays may be so manipulative as to be unduly prejudicial or present a significant danger of confusing the jury.

Final jury instructions. Use of final jury instructions in closing argument is another area where some courts have ground rules to ensure fair use. Showing particularly relevant instructions on the evidence camera as a part of the closing argument is an excellent technique. When the displays of evidentiary exhibits are followed by a key portion of the instructions, the visual impact is particularly powerful. Some courts require that quotes from final jury instructions be of whole sentences in order to prevent words being taken out of context. Generally there are no limitations on the highlighting of particular words or phrases within the complete sentence.

Chapter 9: Objections to Electronic Displays

This chapter sets out a detailed explanation of the objections that may be raised to all types of electronic displays —including those generated with PowerPoint or another slideshow software package—and how to deal with each of them. The material used on an evidence camera is generally uncomplicated and raises few of these objections. Many of these objections refer to slides with computer-generated labels, photos, animations, or colors. However, it is useful to consider "technology" objections in context. Objections are sometimes adapted from one side or the other of the line between evidence camera displays and computer-driven displays, and it is useful to see these objections in their entirety. Also, when one side uses an evidence camera, the other side may counter with computer-generated exhibits. Therefore, the advocate using the evidence camera needs to be prepared across the board with respect to objections to "technology" exhibits.

If the court has a kill switch at the bench that can blank the monitors visible to the jury, then when an objection is made, the court will use that switch to take the exhibit off the monitors. If there is no kill switch available, the normal way to deal with objections is to remove the exhibit from under the evidence camera as soon as an objection is made. If the court overrules the objection, the exhibit can be put back under the evidence camera as the examination of the witness proceeds.

9.1 Objections to evidentiary exhibits

◆

Each evidentiary exhibit must have a foundation that qualifies the exhibit as an appropriate basis for deciding the case. This foundation includes the competence of the witness to testify about the exhibit; the relevance of the exhibit to an issue in the case; the identification of the exhibit distinguishing it from all other things; and the trustworthiness or authentication of the exhibit, sometimes including compliance with the hearsay and original documents rules.

If the exhibit being displayed has been admitted in evidence but has been enhanced in some way, such as with labels, superimposed images, or callouts, it may become an illustrative aid. Even if the underlying exhibit has been admitted, the illustrative aid based on that exhibit can be excluded if the adaptation is unduly prejudicial.

Most objections to exhibits offered in evidence at trial are based on the applicable evidence rules. For purposes of illustration with respect to the various objections that may be available, this discussion refers to the Federal Rules of Evidence. There are some differences in state practice but, because the field of computer-driven visual displays is relatively new, the federal practice offers a useful benchmark.

9.1.1. Objection under an original documents rule

It is sometimes useful to distinguish between (1) evidence that exists in the first instance in physical form (e.g., a handwritten document or standard photo) and is presented electronically, (2) evidence that exists in the first instance in electronic form (e.g., documents created with word processing software, e-mails, photos created with digital cameras) and is converted to paper and offered in evidence in that format; and (3) evidence that exists in the first instance in electronic form (e.g., photos or video created with digital cameras, and digital audio recordings) and is presented electronically.

Evidence that exists in physical form should present no problem under the original documents rule (Fed. R. Evid. 1001–1008) when that evidence is displayed electronically. Lawyers may object that the electronic display of the physical writing is almost always different from the original because the color and resolution of the original cannot be reproduced with absolute accuracy on the monitor or projection screen. For example, in the Unabomber trial, the defense sought to keep the prosecution from displaying the defendant's writings electronically, citing the small differences in color and resolution of the images on the screen (as compared to the paper copies). The objection failed because the purpose of the electronic display was an examination of the textual content of the writings, not their authentication. Once a sufficient foundation is laid, and the exhibit is admitted in evidence, it can be shown electronically in any way the court determines promotes a fair trial. Any enlargement or display of the exhibit itself using courtroom technology should require nothing further by way of exhibit numbering or qualification. The display on the projection screen or monitor is treated the same as the exhibit that has been admitted.

Evidence created in electronic form (for example, a photo taken with a digital camera) and converted to physical form (a printed copy of the photo) for purposes of being admitted in evidence may cause lawyers to raise objections based on the original documents rule. Under Rule 1002, if the exhibit is a writing or a photograph, then the original is required unless, under Rule 1003, a duplicate may be used instead of the original. Electronic files are the "originals" of writings created with word processing software, e-mails, and photographs or videos created with digital cameras. In the case of printouts, Rule 1001(3) defines them as originals. For other uses of digital files, Rule 1001(4) defines a duplicate as anything produced by a process or technique that accurately reproduces the original. The duplicate is admitted under Rule 1003 unless some unfairness can be demonstrated. The burden in that regard is on the opponent. If the digital file is copied to a CD, then the duplicate is the file on the CD. The operating system software process that "copies" digital files is uniformly accepted as accurately reproducing the original. Indeed, it is almost never done any other way.

Evidence created in electronic form and presented in electronic form may have been converted several times in the process of going from the original data file to the data file being presented. For example, a digital photo will be created in a format that is native to the camera used to take the photo. When the file is transferred from the camera to a computer, the file transfer utility software may convert the data to a format preferred by the receiving computer's setup.

> For more on formats and compression, see *Effective Use of Courtroom Technology, A lawyer's Guide to Pretrial and Trial,* Part II (NITA 2002).

When the data file is prepared for presentation in a courtroom, it may be saved to yet another format, usually JPEG, because the smaller file size produced by the JPEG compression capability means the photo can be displayed faster in the courtroom. Technically, under Rule 1001(3), the initial electronic file created by the digital camera is the "original." Each of the subsequent data conversions is a "duplicate" under Rule 1001(4) because it is "produced by ... an electronic re-recording ... which accurately reproduces the original." There is a potential challenge to the status of a compressed file as a duplicate. However, the standard compression, particularly in a well-accepted format like JPEG which was produced by an industry experts group, is unlikely to support a successful objection.

9.1.2 Completeness objection

A legitimate objection may be raised to a visual display that includes only a part of a document taken out of context. In the federal system, Fed. R. Evid. 106 covers writings and recorded statements, including documents and audio and videotapes in lieu of transcriptions. It generally does not apply to photographs and videotapes of scenes or locations relevant to the case or anything else not intended to have the same effect as a writing. However, courts can use their general powers under Rule 611(a) to achieve the same result for materials not covered by Rule 106.

Completeness objection: documents

Presentation software provides enormous flexibility for lawyers to display documents for the fact-finder, whether judge or jury. Pages of documents can be cropped and resized in the same way as photographs. One standard and fair way that documents are presented by experienced lawyers "anchors" the viewer by showing the whole page and the document's exhibit number, and then presents the enhancement of the page that calls attention to its important part.

An issue may arise if counsel elects to show just the portion of the document that the witness is about to explain.

Opposing counsel may object because what is being shown to the jury is just a part of the document. The objection typically has three parts.

First, counsel will argue that the document is a writing and, under Rule 106, the entire page should be displayed and not just a part of it. Counsel may urge that without the whole page in view, there is a danger of confusing or misleading the jury. That is not an insignificant problem. Jurors who are not accustomed to dealing with the kind of paper records at issue in the case may have trouble focusing on segments of documents. By the time they figure out what is being shown, the testimony has already passed to another point.

Second, with computer-generated exhibits (but not with evidence camera exhibits) under Rule 611(a), counsel may argue that this excerpt is intended to limit cross-examination. If the only exhibit available to show on the screen (because this is all one side's computer-generated slide contains) is a portion of the document, then the cross-examiner cannot use the same mode (that is, an enlargement on the screen) as the direct examiner did. In this case, the cross-examiner is limited to the paper copy of the record that may be much less effective than the big screen image. (The same may also be true when a cross-examiner uses just a small portion of a document which might be out of context, and the direct examiner is handcuffed without the full image.) There are some obvious ways around this problem. Effective preparation is one, so that the cross-examiner has digital versions of all the documents. Using the evidence camera to display the paper copy of the entire page on the large screen and zoom in on the relevant portion is another. However, it certainly is true that in direct examination counsel would not normally be allowed to approach the witness with a scissored up portion of a paper copy of a document just to bamboozle an opponent. Using just a portion of a document on a digital exhibit is about the same thing. If the standard method is used, with the whole page displayed, it is a simple operation for opposing counsel to use that slide, with or without the callout, for cross-examination and this problem is obviated. A basic knowledge of presentation software on the part of anyone on the trial team will allow instant enlargement of other portions of the page and competing callouts, and will allow emphasis on whatever aspects the cross-examining counsel believes is necessary.

Third, counsel may argue that the excerpt has been changed from the original and should not be allowed in its changed condition. Because cropping is done on a vertical or horizontal plane, there are sometimes little tags of unwanted and distracting material that cannot be excised through the crop. To get at these pieces, an excerpt may be changed by using small rectangles or circles to block out the unwanted material. When done professionally, a portion of the document background itself would be copied for the blocking rectangles and the match would be exact.

One reason that judges sometimes sustain an objection to this kind of alteration of a cropped segment of a document, even if they are disposed to allow the segment itself, is that some sharp-eyed juror will spot the change and argue about its significance during jury deliberations. This wastes time and diverts the jury from its charge.

Completeness objection: photos

A completeness objection may also arise when photos are cropped. Cropping has always been possible during the enlargement process with regular photos, but digital photos are very easy to change, so more cropping shows up in exhibits prepared with digital files. For example, a photo of a building and its parking lot can be cropped to show just the building.

There is nothing inherently unfair about cropping, but cropping can be used to create images that are, in fact, unfair given the context in which they are used. For example, if the issue is whether the building is a blight on the neighborhood, and the parking lot is full of trash, the photo showing no parking lot at all probably would be unfair.

A completeness objection to a photograph may be based on Rule 611. In response, the court may require that the cropped photo be displayed first in its original state to show the context from which the cropped image was taken.

Because an evidence camera has a defined zoom capability (usually 6x to 10x), it is occasionally necessary to crop a photo so that the zoom capability can be used to get to a very small relevant portion. More often, the proponent simply puts the full photo on the screen and then zooms in on the necessary portion. If there is an objection, the proponent can zoom out to include other portions.

One standard technique for displaying cropped photos with computer-generated displays is to put a small version of the full photo on the display, enlarge the cropped portion, and use connecting lines to show the location from which the cropped portion was taken.

9.1.3 Unfairness objection

For computer-generated exhibits, an "unfairness" objection may arise when a document or photo is displayed differently than it would appear in the original for the purpose of influencing the jury. Similarly, an unfairness objection may be posed when a video is played at a speed different from the normal speed. These objections are not ordinarily relevant to exhibits displayed on an evidence camera.

Unfairness objection: documents

Unfairness objections sometimes arise when documents are displayed without the full margin or color that appears in the original. For example, an insurance policy may have ample white space around its margins although the print is fairly small. If the margins are cropped when the document is displayed, it may give the impression of being more dense and harder to read. Alternatively, the cropped document (having more space to use) may allow a display of a larger type size making the document appear easier to read than it was in the original. The text of the document is complete, but the overall aspect of the document is changed. Normally the reason for cropping the margins of documents is not to create an unfair impression, but to fit more of the document on the screen. Documents are usually 8½ x 11 inches and monitors usually have a height-to-width ratio of 3:4. This means that the full length of the document does not fit well on the typical monitor and cropping the margins, where no text appears, makes the fit somewhat better.

Unfairness objection: photos

Objections may arise when photos have been resized, reshaped, displayed with misleading lighting, or displayed much larger than life.

Resizing is a process in which the photo is made bigger or smaller, perhaps in relation to some other photo, without changing the content of the photo. There is nothing inherently unfair about resizing a photo, but photos of different dimensions can be used to present facts unfairly. A large photo of a small object placed next to a small photo of a large object may suggest unfairly that the two are nearly the same size.

Reshaping is a computer-driven process in which the photo is stretched vertically to make the things it depicts appear "taller," or horizontally to make the things it depicts appear "wider." Reshaping is almost always inherently unfair if size, shape, or distances are in issue. The resulting photo is not an accurate representation of the real thing.

Every presentation software or photo editing software package provides a means to resize photos without distorting them, but when photos are resized they frequently are also distorted. Distortion is usually inadvert because, when presentation software is being used, the tool for resizing a photo is very similar in appearance on the screen to the tool for reshaping the photo.

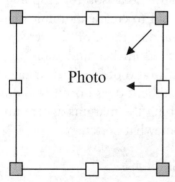 By way of rough illustration, the resizing tool in presentation software is a small square in each corner of the frame that the software puts around a photo. In this illustration, these squares are colored gray. Using the mouse to drag any one of these corner squares will resize the photo but maintain proportionality so that it is not reshaped.

The reshaping tool in presentation software is a small square in the middle of each side of the frame that the software puts around the photo. In this illustration these squares are not colored. Using the mouse to drag any one of these middle squares will reshape and at the same time distort the photo.

In the actual software, all of these small squares look alike (the resizing squares are not gray). So users sometimes drag the middle square (and reshape) when they should have dragged the corner square (and resized).

The fact that distortion can be inadvertent does not diminish its seriousness, but lawyers may not recognize a distorted photo that has been worked on by someone else, so distortion does not always equate with intentional wrongdoing by the lawyer.

The lighting portrayed by nighttime photos may be displayed in a misleading way if an evidence camera is used to show the photo with the wrong contrast and iris settings. Re-creation of nighttime visibility is challenging under most litigation circumstances. When the photo is put on the evidence camera with the iris wide open, the amount of light reaching the camera is maximized. When the contrast is also high, the evidence camera dramatically changes the appearance of what is visible.

Occasionally an unfairness objection is raised about a photo that is enlarged to a size much larger than life. For example, by enlarging a photo of wounds many times more than the actual size of the wound, the importance or effect of the wound might be exaggerated.

9.2 Objections to illustrative aids

The most common objections during testimony at trial—unfairness, leading, argumentative, narrative testimony, assumes facts not in evidence, unsupported opinion, and lay opinion—are logical extensions of the objections that have been directed in the past at large boards displayed on easels or other illustrative aids used with witnesses One useful axiom with respect to objections to visual displays that contain words: What is on the screen is appropriate (and not objectionable) if the lawyer or witness could say those words orally under the circumstances in which the display is introduced. However, with computer-generated materials it is often necessary to "play" the illustrative aid—that is, to see it as it will unfold when shown to the jury—in order to understand the objection in context.

9.2.1. Unfairness objection

An objection based on "unfairness" may arise when an illustrative aid is inaccurate or suggestive in inappropriate ways. Courts sometimes use the benchmarks of Fed. R. Evid. 403—unfair prejudice, confusion of the issues, misleading the jury—in dealing with objections to illustrative aids. If an illustrative aid could be excluded under Rule 403 because the aid's prejudicial effect substantially outweighs its value, then it should be excluded. However, illustrative aids can be excluded, even if the prejudicial effect is not so substantial as to reach the traditional threshold of Rule 403, because they are supposed to be useful, and they cannot be useful if they do not convey information clearly without attendant distraction, unnecessary emphasis, or needless cumulative display.

Unfairness: labels

Labels can show up as a title for the exhibit, or in the margins indicating some aspect of the exhibit, or over a portion of the exhibit. Labels are the first place lawyers generally look for objectionable material.

Labels that are opinion belong only on exhibits that show an appropriate lay opinion pursuant to Fed. R. Evid. 701 or on exhibits sponsored by an expert who is qualified to give the opinion as shown by an appropriate foundation under Rule 702. Labels may contain hearsay and be objectionable on that ground. Labels that state facts should appear only after the fact is in evidence and should not misquote or mischaracterize the evidence. Labels including adjectives and adverbs may be inaccurate because they overstate the facts. Sometimes labels are displayed and then crossed out, indicating an alternative rejected or a path not taken. This is normally acceptable unless it misstates the facts. Labels may give undue emphasis to a portion of the testimony or be cumulative of that testimony and become objectionable on that ground.

Sustainable objections to labels are highly dependent upon the context in which the illustrative aid is offered. Under one set of facts or at one stage of the trial the label may be objectionable, and under another set of facts or later in the trial the same label may be entirely proper.

Unfairness: text treatments

Text "treatments" are methods for emphasizing particularly relevant portions of text embedded in a relatively long text document. Treatments are usually boxes, underlines, circles, bold and italic typefaces, and callouts added to a page of text.

Text treatments can be unfair if used in a way that might mislead or confuse the jury about the original document. For example, words in very fine print may be enlarged and put in large bold capital letters. This may be done to give the impression that the information was emphasized in the original document when in fact it was not. This problem is largely avoided if the original document is displayed at the same time as the text treatment, and standard methods for emphasis or callouts are followed.

Unfairness: colors

With computer-generated illustrative aids, color usually appears on the background of the slide (behind all of the objects or writing on the slide), or on an object on the slide as a way of setting off or emphasizing the content (such as a rectangle or circle on which words have been written), or as a screen that makes objects on the slide appear or disappear.

Background color, even if lacking in taste or articulated purpose, is rarely objectionable in and of itself. Lawyers sometimes use background color to indicate the subject matter of the slide. For example, the exhibits that have to do with liability might have a dark blue background and the exhibits that have to do with damages might have a dark green background. Background color may indicate the relative importance of an exhibit. The most important exhibits may have no background color at all.

Color used on objects or exhibits may be objectionable when the purpose is to suggest linkages that may not exist in fact and for which there is no foundation. For example, a photo of a piece of equipment painted yellow may be admitted in evidence and displayed on a large screen. The lawyer may then have exhibits that use the color yellow, displayed immediately following the display of the enlarged photo, to suggest that other things are a part of this equipment when there is no foundation for that link. Similarly, a company may be labeled with a color and then a person not connected to the company may be labeled with the same color to suggest a conspiracy or identity of purpose. Or, perhaps more commonly, a symbol on a diagram indicating a traffic light may be colored red or green when the status of the light is not established by testimony.

Unlike permanent foam-board exhibits that were their predecessors in the courtroom, computer-generated exhibits can be changed very readily, even on the spot, usually with only a few keystrokes. If there is a problem with a particular color, the slide can be retrieved, a color palette with many shades can be displayed, and the offending color can be changed instantly without changing anything else on the slide. It is an unusual case, therefore, where a party will be prejudiced by last-minute changes in color required by the court.

Unfairness: intervals

Time lines are frequently used in cases in which a sequence of dates or times is important to the case theory. Most time lines include intervals, marked off in some way, representing the amount of time that passed between events. If the intervals on the time line, when measured, do not accurately (that is, proportionally) represent the amount of time that actually passed, then there may be an objection based on presenting misleading and possibly confusing information to the jury.

A time line is an illustrative aid, and therefore will not be sent to the jury room during deliberations. For that reason, a relaxed standard about accuracy may be appropriate so long as the distortions are not large or the exact time interval between events is not at issue. In some cases, it would be difficult for the designer of the time line to get all the information on one exhibit with a type size that could be read. However, the use of a computer in design work makes it very easy to get time intervals exactly correct. If the intervals are not a true representation, it might be better to indicate that with a break in the line that is the axis on which the dates are indicated.

9.2.2 Leading objection

The traditional objection to leading questions is directed at lawyers' statements that suggest the desired answer to the witness. Illustrative aids may have content or markings that will lead the witness in reciting testimony. With fact witnesses, the objection to leading the witness is usually made with respect to labels or bullet points that appear on the screen before the witness has testified to a particular fact.

Illustrative aids that accompany expert testimony are often prepared for this very purpose, so that the expert provides an explanation that is organized and well paced. They are less objectionable on these grounds, however, if the expert prepared the illustrative aids and determined their content. The expert cannot improperly suggest the answer to himself or herself, and the leading of an expert in his or her area of expertise may be allowed if for the purpose of clarifying the testimony.

9.2.3 Argumentative objection

Objections that illustrative aids are argumentative (and therefore should not be displayed to the jury) can arise during opening statements, expert testimony, and direct and cross-examination of fact witnesses. With respect to opening statement, the prohibition against argument is inherent in the purpose of creating a context for the jury's understanding. Argument does not further that purpose, and therefore is improper during opening statement. With respect to witness examination, the objection is generally grounded in the proposition that testimony is for the purpose of eliciting information, not for arguing the case to the jury.

Illustrative aids that support an opening or witness examination may be argumentative in the same general ways as oral statements. The objection is most often directed to the wording on a label. Labels including adjectives and adverbs may be argumentative. Labels stating relationships (something happened because something else occurred first; the problem was due to a particular circumstance) may also draw this objection.

The design of a graphic display may also draw an objection as argumentative. For example, the typical relationship chart shows a flow from one event to another by having the arrows appear one after another before reaching the bottom-line conclusion. (See examples in *PowerPoint® 2002 for Litigators* (NITA 2003) and *Argument Slides* (NITA 2003).)This design is appropriate for final argument, but occasionally finds its way into the examination of an expert witness under the guise of explaining the expert's work.

9.2.4 Assuming facts not in evidence objection

The traditional objection in this area seeks to disqualify a question that assumes a fact not in evidence. The basis for the objection is that the answer given by the witness to such a question cannot be fairly used by a jury in arriving at a decision in the case. Illustrative aids used in the direct examination of witnesses sometimes cross into this area. This may happen when a statement, photo, or other material is displayed that purports to present a fact that has not already been admitted in evidence or at least is not within the competence or knowledge of the witness with whom the slides are used.

In the federal system, experts are allowed, under Fed. R. Evid. 703, to rely on facts or data not admissible in evidence. The question arises, with respect to displays used by an expert to explain his or her opinion, whether a slide can include statements, photos, or other data not admissible in evidence as a helpful means of presenting the expert's opinion to the jury or assisting the jury in understanding the expert's opinion. Pursuant to the December 2000 changes in Rule 703, while these facts may be used as a basis for the expert's opinion, if the data or facts are not otherwise admissible, they may not be communicated to the jury "unless the court determines that their probative value in assisting the jury to evaluate the expert's opinion substantially outweighs their prejudicial effect." As a result, such facts or data should not normally appear on an illustrative aid until the court has ruled on their admissibility.

9.2.5. Foundation (unsupported opinion) objection

Expert witnesses are the most frequent users of illustrative aids presented with courtroom technology. Lawyers who prepare well for a complicated case will use jury research to identify the case themes that are likely to cause a representative jury to decide issues in the client's favor. Sometimes these themes show up in the displays that the expert sponsors even though the expert has no facts at hand or knowledge, skill, experience, training, or education that would provide a foundation for direct testimony. An objection to this kind of display is often stated as "argument," because the display is in effect arguing the client's cause.

9.2.6 Lay opinion objection

The titles, labels, or other text on an illustrative aid used with a lay witness may be objectionable under Rule 701 if the illustrative aid includes words or phrases that are fairly characterized as opinion or inference and do not meet the requirements in the rule that the opinion be: "(a) rationally based on the perception of the witness [and] (b) helpful to a clear understanding of the witness' testimony or the determination of a fact in issue...."

9.2.7 Objections to digitally altered photographs

Digitally altered photographs have been changed in some respect from the "original" using software tools. Such photos may be offered in evidence, in which case a witness usually will testify that the photograph is an accurate representation of something about which the witness has personal knowledge. Occasionally this kind of photo is offered as an illustrative aid, to assist in the presentation of the testimony.

If the altered photo is offered in evidence, the proponent will argue that it makes no difference if alterations have been made as long as the witness testifies that the photo in its current state is an accurate representation of what the witness observed. In the federal system, under Rule 901, if the witness has the necessary personal knowledge, that foundation will suffice. The cross-examiner then has the burden to point out the effects of the alterations.

The opponent may argue that the traditional Rule 901 formulation is not sufficient with respect to a photograph that has been digitally altered. When the witness looks at a photo, the witness does not (and perhaps cannot) verify all of the component parts of the photo. The witness confirms some of the major components and assumes that all of the remaining components are all right. With traditional photos, that foundation sufficed because, although it has always been possible to alter photos, it was unlikely that part of the photo would be right and part of it would be wrong. In addition, most changes to a photo, such as airbrushing, required specialized professional equipment and occurred in ways that could be detected. With digital photos, any part of the image can be changed electronically in ways that are quite hard for the unaided eye to detect. The changes can be made with software that is commercially available at very low cost, and both small and large changes can be made by anyone who can read an instruction manual. Therefore, the argument goes, unless the witness can verify every aspect of the photo from personal knowledge, the foundation is insufficient. And such verification would take up too much time to be worthwhile.

Many digitally altered photos are just as useful as drawings, some more so, in orienting the jurors to the scene of an accident, the layout of an industrial plant, certain environmental impacts, and many other purposes for which they have been permitted as illustrative aids. Some alterations, such as changing the contrast, do not alter any of the objects depicted by the photo but make the photo easier for the viewer to see details. The fact of the digital alteration, standing alone, is not enough to prohibit their use.

Chapter 10: Use with Other Technology

An evidence camera can be used as the sole item of courtroom technology supporting a trial, or it can be used in conjunction with other technology. The choices, with respect to technology support, generally depend on the issues in the case, the likely length of the trial, the types of exhibits that will be used, and the court's views about technology.

10.1 Matching technology to exhibits

This section covers the best way to display particular exhibits. Deciding early in the pretrial process on the equipment to be used to present visual displays will save a great deal of time and effort over the life of the case. In most litigation, there is some chance of settlement and this often causes lawyers to delay making decisions about trial. In a situation where a lawyer plans to use technology at trial, at least preliminary decisions need to be made considerably in advance of trial to have any hope of an orderly preparation.

The first agenda item is an assessment of the likely categories of evidence to be offered, as some equipment is better for particular displays than others.

Exhibit type	Best input	Easiest output
Photographs	Evidence camera	Projector and screen
Charts, graphs	Laptop computer	Small individual juror monitors
Text documents	Laptop computer	Projector and screen
Maps, drawings, diagrams	Evidence camera	Projector and screen
Small objects	Evidence camera	Projector and screen
X-rays, CAT scans, MRI images	Evidence camera	Large high-resolution monitor
Time lines	Laptop computer	Projector and screen
Tables, printouts	Evidence camera	Projector and screen
Videotape excerpts	Laptop computer	Large high-resolution monitor
Sound recordings	Laptop computer	High-resolution audio speakers
Animations, simulations	Laptop computer	Projector and screen

If more than one category of evidence is expected, then combinations of equipment may be required. Both an evidence camera and a laptop computer can provide input for either a projector and screen setup or large or small monitor setups using a switch to go back and forth between the input devices. Some newer evidence cameras come with built-in switches for this purpose.

§10.1

The next item on the agenda is a visit to the courtroom where the case will be tried. This is not always a simple matter. In some jurisdictions, there is only one courtroom so that determining the site of the trial is not a problem. In other jurisdictions, however, judges move from courtroom to courtroom so, even if the case is assigned to a particular judge, lawyers have no guarantee that the trial will wind up in a particular courtroom. If the clerk's office knows that the trial would benefit from the use of technology, sometimes a particular courtroom can be reserved.

If the courtroom has equipment installed on a permanent basis, the trial lawyer needs a list of the makes and models of each item of equipment—monitors, projectors, screens, evidence cameras, annotation equipment, audio equipment—and the location of the plug for a laptop or other controls. The trial lawyer also needs a diagram of the courtroom showing the location of the principal fixtures (bench, counsel tables, jury box, reporter's table, clerk's desk), the distances from one to another, the location of each electrical outlet, and the location of windows and the permanently installed lights. This information will permit an informed assessment of how (and whether) to use the court's existing equipment. If a lawyer wants to bypass the court's equipment and import something else, it is always a good idea to make that request very early. See chapter 7 on pretrial preparations.

10.2 Range of technology choices

Occasionally the choice of technology is dictated by what the other side plans to use (see section 7.3 on disclosure) or other special needs of the case. This section discusses briefly the available options. For more details, see *Effective Use of Courtroom Technology: A Lawyer's Guide to Pretrial and Trial* (NITA 2002).

10.2.1 Laptop computer with retrieval and presentation software

The laptop is the most convenient personal computer for courtroom use because of its portability and built-in monitor. Many laptops have just as much functionality, storage (also called memory, disk drive, hard disk, floppy disk, or external disk), and retrieval capacity as ordinary desktop models and provide all of the necessary connections to external devices. A laptop displays images on its own built-in monitor as well as on any external monitors to which it is connected.

The most basic use of a computer in a courtroom setting is for retrieval of images of exhibits to be displayed on the monitors or via the projector to which the computer is connected. Every image of an exhibit is stored in a named file, and when the proper name is entered, the computer's operating system software locates the correct file and displays the first page of its content. If the file names match the exhibit numbers, a software search program can be implemented so that, for example, when the designation PX113 is typed on the computer keyboard, Plaintiff's Exhibit 113 will be displayed. When using digital displays, it is common to number both evidentiary exhibits and illustrative aids as "exhibits" in order to make a better record.

Alternatively, a touch screen retrieval system can be used. A touch screen is a special computer monitor with a surface that is sensitive to touch. The exhibits are listed on the display on this monitor, usually by number, and when the lawyer wants a particular exhibit, he or she touches the number of the exhibit, and it appears.

A third method is the bar code reader, a small handheld device that translates a bar code—on a sticker placed on the lawyer's notes, an exhibit list, or a duplicate set of exhibits—into the necessary commands to the computer to locate and display the correct file. When the lawyer wants a particular document on the screen, he or she passes the bar code reader over the bar code, and the document appears.

Computers also create and display illustrative aids by combining an exhibit with enhancements that make the content of the exhibit easier to understand or by producing bullet lists, charts, graphs, and diagrams. This is done with presentation software that generates, as well as retrieves visual displays. This kind of software can highlight and enlarge relevant portions of documents or photos, juxtapose text from two or more pages, and add explanatory titles and labels. Two categories are used in courts: standard presentation software that has sufficient capability for courtroom use; and high-end software developed specially for courtroom use.

The standard software is usually Microsoft's PowerPoint or Corel's Corel Presentations. Lawyers often use the terms "PowerPoint slides" or "slide show" to describe the visual displays they plan to present (even if the software is something other than Microsoft's). This software creates visual displays that can be changed readily, but generally the changes must be done before the display is used and cannot be done "on the fly." Either PowerPoint or Corel Presentations can be used in the courtroom to display exhibits and both software packages have easy controls for those purposes.

The high-end specialized software includes Sanction, from Verdict Systems; Trial Pro, from Idea, Inc.; and Trial Director, from InData Corp. Other proprietary software is provided by litigation consulting firms as a part of their package of services. The high-end software includes all of the capabilities of the standard presentation software but also allows changes to be made as the exhibit is being displayed. For example, if the display includes a segment of document text, but does not include any enlargement of the text, the high-end software allows the user to pull the text out and enlarge it on the spot with a simple mouse command.

A laptop computer can be used to display digitized videotaped transcripts of depositions, to play digitized audio files, and to present complex animations. These displays typically involve very large files that were created on much larger systems. Newer laptops have the storage capability to accommodate these files and to get them to the monitors or projection screen in the courtroom without undue delay. As an alternative, large files can be run from a CD. In a case where there are many video clips from depositions that might be used in cross-examination, for example, the cross-examining lawyer might have one CD for each adverse witness.

A laptop computer can operate either independently or with the courtroom audio and video system. If a courtroom has no audio system, the laptop can be cabled to high-performance speakers that have been brought to the courtroom. With external speakers, using an amplifier between the laptop and the speakers produces higher quality audio. If the courtroom has no visual display system, the laptop can be cabled to a digital projector that will put the image on a large projection screen. The laptop can also be cabled to monitors brought to the courtroom for the occasion. If the laptop is operating within a courtroom audio or video system, a computer interface plug is provided by the court. This plug may be located at counsel table or at an integrated lectern. The interface, which varies depending on how the courtroom is equipped and cabled, connects to the courts amplified sound system and amplifies the video signals as necessary to deliver quality images to the court's display devices.

10.2.2 Annotation equipment

Annotation equipment makes a low-key but substantial contribution to presenting exhibits by allowing a lawyer or witness to mark up images being generated by an evidence camera or laptop computer, whether displayed on a monitor or projection screen. This facilitates pointing out what is significant in the display, directing attention to a particular aspect, or drawing connecting lines to compare or contrast features so that the presentation of opening statements, witness testimony, and closing arguments can move along more expeditiously.

Three kinds of equipment are available to direct attention to particular aspects of the images on monitors and projection screens: the touch screen, the light pen and the telestrator. Each device produces essentially the same output. The "draw" capability creates an overlay that appears on top of the image but does not change it. The overlay may be a line or a static pointer arrow. The color and size of the overlay can be changed using the annotation equipment controls, and the overlay can be erased in whole or in part as the explanation proceeds.

A touch screen monitor is a computer monitor with a surface that responds to touch by a finger or stylus. It is cabled so that the drawing on its surface can be projected to all other monitors or to the projector. The touch screen is the most intuitive of the annotation alternatives because the user is interacting directly with the image on the monitor. This capability can be added to either a CRT (traditional) monitor or an LCD (flat panel) monitor.

A light pen enables the user to move a special stylus device across the surface of a full-sized computer monitor to create the overlay. This type of annotation tool is often known as the "John Madden pen" after the well-known television sports commentator who highlights and diagrams football plays as an aid to his game commentary. The light pen sometimes causes difficulty because it must be held almost exactly at right angles to the surface of the monitor in order to work properly, and requires practice because most people do not write that way. This annotation tool can be used only with a CRT monitor.

A telestrator is a tablet with a stylus and touch controls; the tablet is connected between the evidence camera (or computer) generating the image and the monitors or projector displaying the image. Any motion of the stylus on the tablet is translated into an overlay on the image transmitted to the monitors or projector. This equipment is more difficult to operate because the user must look at the monitor while marking on the tablet. The eye–hand coordination necessary to accomplish this comes quite easily, but it feels counterintuitive at the outset and requires some practice. The telestrator can be used with a CRT (traditional) monitor or an LCD (flat panel) monitor, as well as with a projector.

Presentation software, discussed above with laptop computers, usually has an annotation capability that works in the same general manner as the annotation equipment described above except that the control is the computer's mouse. For that reason, the software alternative is limited to annotation of illustrative aids being presented with that software and annotation can be done only from the computer that is controlling the presentation.

10.2.3 Color video printer

The use of annotation options necessitates being able to make a record of the annotation, when necessary. Prepared illustrative aids can be preserved for the record on a CD, but on-the-spot annotations change those prepared materials. A verbal description is both cumbersome and inadequate. A printout of anything that is currently being displayed on a monitor or projection screen can be made conveniently with a video printer that is specially adapted for this purpose. The printout includes the image itself and any annotations from the touch screen, light pen, or telestrator. The output from the printer is usually 3½ x 5 inches, which is sufficient to record what was before the jury.

A specialized video printer works better in a courtroom environment than an ordinary computer printer because the controls are simplified, marks made with any of the three annotation tools (touch screen, light pen, and telestrator) can be recorded, and the delay between the request for a printout and the appearance of the finished product is much shorter. Making a print this way requires pushing only one button and waiting about 45 seconds. The video printer is specialized equipment not optimized for making a permanent record. Its prints tend to fade over time. However, copying the print on any standard copier will produce a record that will last.

10.2.4 Audio system

Some courtroom technology—computers, videoconference equipment, laser disk players, VCRs, and audiotape players—relies on sound as well as visual presentations. Audio is also important for telephone conferencing, telephone and infrared interpreting systems, and electronic sound recording.

If a court has no audio system at all, lawyers can use simple speaker systems to project audio adequately for most purposes. Battery-powered computer speakers will provide sound for very short, non-critical tasks. Small quality speakers produced by a number of manufacturers, powered from wall plugs, are much better. For a small courtroom, these speakers will get the job done with respect to the sound components of most exhibits or deposition records. Using an amplifier between the laptop and the speakers may be necessary if the acoustics of the courtroom are not very good.

A court's audio system usually includes built-in speakers located to maximize clarity of sound given the acoustic characteristics of the room. The audio system may also include microphones at the bench, witness stand, and counsel table to reinforce the oral exchanges in the courtroom. The type and placement of microphones is particularly important for an effective audio system. Some courts have upgraded audio including microphones equipped with mute buttons at the bench and counsel table, a white or pink noise generator at the bench to muffle the conversation during bench conferences, a connection between the sidebar area of the bench and the court reporter (so that the reporter does not have to move the steno equipment in order to record bench conferences), infrared transmitters to deliver enhanced audio for the hearing impaired or those needing translations, and connections into the audio system for laptops and CD and DVD players.

10.2.5 Telephone interpreting system

The telephone interpreting system provides interpreting services from English to foreign languages and vice versa for short proceedings such as pretrial hearings, initial appearances, arraignments, motion hearings, and probation and pretrial services interviews. Defendants and witnesses hear the foreign language translation through telephone handsets or headsets. Others in the courtroom hear the English translation of foreign language testimony through a speaker telephone or the court's audio system.

Two telephone lines are used. One line is connected to a digital conference phone. The second is connected to a conventional telephone handset or headset. On one line, the interpreter listens to the English or the foreign language from the courtroom via the conference phone. The interpreter then interprets into the foreign language or English, whichever is required, and directs by way of a hand switch the interpretation to either the conventional receiver or the conference phone, whichever is required. Good courtroom audio is important to this system so that the interpreter and all participants can hear all of the relevant speech.

10.2.6 Electronic whiteboard

The electronic whiteboard has two sets of functions: first, it replaces the traditional blackboard as a surface that can be written on and erased; second, it replaces the touch screen as a surface that can both display computer images and direct commands to the computer. Specific makes and models of electric whiteboard equipment have one or both functions.

When the white board is used as a writing surface, dry-erase marking pens in black, blue, green, and red produce diagrams, drawings, lists of points, and any other function of a blackboard or flip chart. It is more functional than those older alternatives because marks can be erased and changed at any time. The whiteboard may have a pressure sensitive surface on which the user writes. Or it may use markers that are embedded with tracking devices. With either kind of board, sensors in or around the board pick up and track the position, movement, and color of the pen. A personal computer records what is written on the whiteboard (including what has been erased), so the information can be saved for later use. A color printer attached to the system can provide printouts.

The image displayed on the whiteboard can also be transmitted simultaneously to all of the monitors in the courtroom. This permits the witness to step down from the stand and draw with the markers without having to reposition the whiteboard so everyone in the courtroom can see it. The witness does not have to stand in a particular place so as not to block the view of the drawing. A whiteboard can be used like a traditional paper flip chart to go from one "page" of markings backward and forward to other pages.

If the content of a Web site or other computer-generated material is at issue, an interactive white board can project the screen display shown on a laptop or other computer and, with touch screen capability, can operate the display as if it were the computer. For example, if it is necessary to "press" a particular button to get a Web site to go to a location, the lawyer can touch the image of the button on the whiteboard, and the button will be activated in the same way as if it had been "clicked" on using a mouse. Similarly, if a series of slides is to be shown, the lawyer can touch the controls for forward and back to move through the slides.

The screen is typically 4 feet high and 5 feet wide and rests on a stand. This equipment is designed to work with computers. It does not work with directly connected evidence cameras.

Currently available models include the Ideaboard from 3M's Visual Systems Division and the SmartBoard made by Smart Technologies, Inc.

10.2.7 Integrated lectern

An integrated lectern incorporates the equipment, connections, and controls necessary for a lawyer to operate most of the courtroom technology from one position. The lectern usually includes an evidence camera, connections for the lawyer's laptop computer to drive displays on the courtroom's monitors or projection screen, annotation equipment, a color video printer, a microphone, and connections to the court's sound system and videoconference system. The lectern may also include two VCRs, one to view exhibits that are VHS and S-VHS tapes, and the other to record the displays on the monitors in the courtroom. Telephone conferences and videoconferences can be initiated and controlled from the lectern depending on the court's practice in these regards. The lectern may ride on casters so it can face the bench or the jury box. These units may be a part of the court's equipment, or may be rented for the occasion by one of the parties.

10.2.8 Videoconference equipment

A videoconference is a televised telephone conference call. In a regular telephone conference call, only audio signals are sent back and forth on the telephone lines connecting the two parties. In a video conference call, both audio and video signals are sent back and forth on the data transmission lines together with the information necessary to synchronize the audio with the video. Video signals require more transmission capacity than audio signals, so higher capacity lines are needed to carry them successfully.

In videoconferencing terms, there is a "near side" or "local site," in this case the courtroom, and a "far side" or "remote site," which is the room or office from which the participant who is not in the courtroom will be appearing. The far side may be a courtroom in another jurisdiction, a prison, a university, a private office equipped for videoconferencing, or a commercial center where a videoconference room has been rented on an hourly basis. Like a telephone conference call, a videoconference can be conducted between two points or many points.

- Cameras. The video signals at each end are generated by one or more video cameras. In the courtroom, the video camera or cameras are usually in fixed locations. At the remote location (or "far side"), the video camera usually is a small portable model placed on top of the monitor. In the courtroom, the cameras may have a fixed focus, or they may be voice-activated and focus on whomever is speaking. At the far side, the camera may have a fixed focus, or it may be under the control of the courtroom so that its focus can be shifted around the room as the court directs.

- Monitors. The video signals at each end are displayed on one or more monitors. There may be a single large monitor in the courtroom, placed near or above the witness stand where everyone in the courtroom can see it, or the video may be displayed on small, built-in monitors in the jury box and the other monitors at the bench and on counsel table. The monitor at the far side is generally placed opposite the witness. The participants in the courtroom can see the witness, usually a head shot; and the witness can see the courtroom, usually a head shot of the lawyer who is doing the questioning. Most portable units are equipped with 32-inch display monitors. In situations where the camera and monitors are built-in, large plasma displays are often used.

- Microphones. The audio signals at each end are generated by microphones. The type and placement of microphones is particularly important as poor audio quality is often the most aggravating aspect of the use of videoconference systems. Each courtroom or videoconference room has acoustic characteristics that need to be taken into account. Microphones come in many sizes and shapes—lapel clip-on, arm-mounted, and desk-top—to accommodate these problems. Positioning is also important. The microphones should be placed so that shuffling of papers and other random noises at counsel table or on the bench are not transmitted.

- Speakers. The audio signals at each end are delivered by speakers. The audio for the courtroom end is usually directed into the courtroom audio system with fixed speakers, but can be directed to any speakers. The audio for the far end usually is delivered through speakers in the monitor or small auxiliary speakers. The participants in the courtroom can hear the witness; and the witness can hear whoever is speaking in the courtroom.

- Data lines. The connection between the two ends of the conference—the courtroom and the distant location—is through special high speed telephone lines. These may be ISDN (Integrated Services Digital Network) lines, cable, DSL (Digital Subscriber Line), or the higher capacity T1 or fiber optic lines. Satellite transmission may also be used. Higher capacity costs more, but delivers the transmission with less delay, more lifelike motion, and better audio.

- Codec. The video and audio signals at each end are directed to a codec (coder-decoder) that processes the signals going to and coming from the telephone lines into a format that the telephone lines and display equipment can accept. The codec coordinates video signals and audio signals so that viewers at both ends see video that matches the audio they hear.

- Enhanced audio. Videoconferencing almost always requires enhancement of the court's audio system. The most significant addition is echo cancellation equipment. When sound from the far side, for example, is broadcast in the courtroom, the courtroom's audio equipment will pick up that sound and send it back through the codec to the far side. All codecs have built-in echo cancellation, but in larger rooms an external echo canceller is required. (If the courtroom is equipped with a built-in audio conferencing unit, the codec audio can be routed through that.) Echo cancellation equipment detects duplicates in the sound transmissions (the echo back to one side or the other of the sound they are sending out) and cancels them out. Without good echo cancellation, the pause in the courtroom (after the person on the far side has spoken) must be longer before the effects of the "echo" in the courtroom are overcome. Long pauses make the effective communication between the courtroom and the remote location more difficult. Echo cancellation equipment is relatively costly, but highly necessary for high-quality videoconferencing.

Commercial videoconferencing centers exist in most urban areas and can be rented for $100 to $150 per hour. They provide the equipment necessary to connect to the court's system and the data lines for transmission. It is also possible to rent videoconferencing equipment to set up in any private location, but the telephone company will take several weeks to install the necessary data lines.

10.2.9 Real-time reporting

Real-time reporting is a service provided by specially trained court reporters who use software that matches the keystrokes on a stenograph machine to corresponding entries in a database and thereby "translates" the keystrokes into words. This software is marketed to court reporters by several competing software publishers. The court reporter's computer assembles the product of these software operations and dispatches them immediately to any connected monitors. Real-time reporters take extensive training in order to be able to produce relatively clean transcripts using this technology.

Voice writer reporters who record proceedings by speaking into a stenomask can also produce real-time transcripts. Speech recognition software translates the voice input to digital format, the digital signals are matched to entries in a database, and the resulting English words are brought to the monitors in the courtroom in a transcript format.

Real-time reporting requires cabling from the reporter's computer to a junction box that routes the signals. Cabling from the junction box reaches all the receiving monitors or computers.

There are two levels of real-time service. Either of these levels of service may be made available only to the court, which is currently more common, or may be provided to counsel tables or in other locations in the courtroom.

The first level of service delivers the transcript to any authorized computer monitor as it comes from the reporter's computer. In some courtrooms, monitors for the basic service are provided by the court. The transcript scrolls down the screen as the reporter proceeds. The transcript is stored on the reporter's computer and the controls remain with the reporter. Anyone with access to a monitor can see as much of the previous and current transcript as fits on the screen. No viewer can stop, start, or affect the transcript. If a judge or lawyer needs to refer to earlier testimony, the reporter must scroll back to that spot in order for it to be displayed on the monitors.

The second level of service delivers the court reporter's output to a laptop computer loaded with special software designed to make the displayed text more usable. In nearly all courtrooms, to gain access to this level of service, lawyers must provide their own laptops and real-time "receiving" software. The transcript is delivered to the receiving computer (and displayed on that computer's monitor) as it comes from the reporter's computer. However, in this case, the transcript is stored on the receiving computer. The controls are with the user of the receiving computer. This user can now scroll backward to prior testimony, add private notes directly to his or her copy of the transcript, add color to portions of the testimony that are useful with respect to certain topics, highlight portions of the witness's testimony for later reference, and search the transcript for particular words or phrases. This level of service also makes an unedited written transcript available immediately because any receiving laptop can copy the file to a disk, print out the file, or send the file via e-mail to some distant computer. The current software packages used by lawyers with this level of service are: Summation Realtime (used with Summation Blaze) from Summation Legal Technologies Inc.; LiveNote from LiveNote Inc.; CaseView from Stenograph LLC; and e-Binder from RealLegal, Inc.

10.2.10 Digital audio reporting

Digital audio recording uses a computer-based system, working with sound system components, to create digital files representing spoken words. This is similar to making a tape recording of the proceeding, except that the sound is stored in digital form on computers and can be transferred to CDs. The principal systems are FTR Gold manufactured by FTR Ltd.; CourtSmart from CourtSmart Digital Systems Inc.; and CourtFlow from BCB Voice Systems, a division of Voice IQ, Inc.

The system is monitored by a court operator who creates a log including the name of the case, the names and addresses of the lawyers, and the name of each speaker. The operator may also record keywords in an examination. The log entries are keyed to the numeric count on the recorder and are synchronized to time stamps on the digital audio recording. The operator makes an index of the entries. All of the entries by the operator can be searched.

This system also has two levels of service. The first is simply a replacement for traditional analog audiotape recording systems and creates a more useful record. Storage of the record is easier, access to the record and playback takes less time, the system can be integrated with other digital systems, and the record can be transmitted electronically to court offices and transcriptionists. If operating correctly, the audio quality is higher than four-channel audio recording. This first level of service creates only an audio record, not a written transcript. However, it allows judges and lawyers to take personal notes which are hidden and not published when the official transcript is prepared. These notes are searchable by the author along with the operator's notes.

The second level of service is in the experimental stage. It combines digital audio with speech recognition technology to produce a written record as well as an audio record. The output works in the same way as real-time reporting. As the testimony is given, the transcript scrolls down the monitors authorized to receive the output so that viewers can see the transcript as it is being created. A printed transcript can be created at any time that, like an unedited real-time transcript, contains errors made by the software in recognizing certain words. Speech recognition technology is currently not as accurate as real-time stenographic transcriptions because of software limitations in dealing with the speed at which people speak in a courtroom, the unusual terms they use in speaking about specialized subjects, and the various accents and dialects that may be present. However, lawyers may request permission from the court to bring this equipment into the courtroom for the purpose of having a real-time transcript available during trial, either because no certified real-time reporter is available or because the client cannot afford the currently scheduled court reporter fees.

10.2.11 Internet connections

Internet connections allow computers used in the courtroom to reach the Internet through an Internet service provider.

Court staff who work in the courtroom typically access the Internet through their building LAN connections. If these connections have been provided, the bench and staff locations will have been wired for this purpose.

Lawyers access the Internet through telephone lines at counsel table. For security reasons, lawyers cannot connect to the court's internal network and use the court's gateway to get to the Internet. The telephone lines at counsel table may be standard lines of the kind that would also be used for voice communications, or special digital subscriber lines (DSL) optimized to carry data at high volumes. These connections may also be through cable or satellite depending on the particular circumstances of the court's location and wiring. The visible part of the connection is a small plug outlet (that may be built into the walls or furniture) like the standard outlets used in homes and offices. Some courts require that these lines be activated by the lawyer so that the lawyer is charged per minute by the telephone company for using the lines.

With an Internet connection at counsel table, lawyers can use e-mail and instant messaging for communications to and from their offices, do research, provide real-time transcripts to colleagues and co-counsel in distant locations, and receive needed materials from other lawyers, investigators, or experts. For example, an expert in an office in a distant city may watch the real-time transcript as the trial unfolds and communicate with the lawyer in the courtroom via instant messaging. The ability to tap into Internet-accessed legal research databases may be of assistance to the court as well.

Court reporters may use the internal system to communicate from the courtroom to their staff in another room in the courthouse, but use the same kind of external system as the lawyers use to reach their offices outside the courthouse. With an Internet connection at the reporter's table, the court reporter can transmit real-time transcripts to support staff who are cleaning up words and phrases that the real-time database could not locate, and the Internet connection allows this process to move faster. The support staff can also communicate with the reporter in the courtroom to make adjustments to the vocabulary stored in the database so that the output will become even more accurate.

At times, courts have made Internet connections available so that media and legal Web sites can carry real-time transcripts to inform the public when the press of public inquiry requires. Requests for these connections usually raise issues relating to the privacy interests of witnesses and parties.

Chapter 11: Troubleshooting

An evidence camera is a sturdy, simple, and extraordinarily reliable unit. Once it is hooked up and operating, very few things can go wrong.

11.1 Cautions for avoiding trouble

An evidence camera will last longer if users heed a few guidelines that almost all manufacturers recommend.

Installation

Do not install an evidence camera in—

- Hot locations or near an open flame or fire
- Very humid locations, or where water or moisture can get on the equipment
- Very dusty locations
- Areas exposed to direct sunlight
- Areas exposed to salt spray
- Anywhere close to flammable solvents

Power cord

The power cord should not be walked on or pinched by objects placed on or against the cord. Disconnect the power cord when the unit is not in use to protect it from power surges.

Ventilation

The evidence camera unit has slots and openings in the cabinet to ensure that it does not overheat while operating. Be sure that these openings are not blocked or covered.

Outlets

Do not overload wall outlets or extension cords. This risks fire or electric shock.

Very bright light sources

Do not point the camera directly at the sun or another close-by very bright light source. This can damage the camera.

Fluorescent lights

The upper lights become very hot after they have been in use for a short time. Be careful not to touch them. Do not store the unit until the lights have cooled down.

Power switch

After turning the unit off, wait at least 30 seconds before turning it on again. Turning it on too rapidly can cause malfunction.

Storage

Store the unit in a horizontal position. If it is left vertically, it may be knocked over and damaged.

11.2 Troubleshooting

Two sets of troubleshooting guides are set out below: a list of the principal sources of problems; and a list of symptoms with problem-solving moves.

11.2.1 Principal problems

Bulb broken: If someone drops the unit while running up the courthouse steps, a bulb may break. Normally bulbs have a life of 1,000 to 3,000 hours, and they are not a problem in regular use. Make sure there is a spare.

Lens cover on: The camera lens has a cover to protect it when not in use. If the lens cover is on, no light will reach the camera and the screen will be black. Take the lens cover off.

Iris knob turned down: The iris knob adjusts the amount of light reaching the camera. If the iris knob is turned down, thus reducing the amount of light reaching the camera, the screen looks black. Turn the iris knob back up.

Nonfunctioning electrical outlet: Courtroom electrical outlets may be nonfunctioning or only partially functioning. Sometimes courtroom maintenance is so poor that one outlet after another has become nonfunctioning over the years until the entire courtroom is down to just one operational outlet. In some instances, outlets have been turned off for some purpose and never turned on again.

Batteries kaput: If a remote is used, every trial week should start with fresh batteries in the remote. Batteries can expire at inopportune times, but the remote is designed for at least 40 hours of continuous operation so if the batteries are fresh you will make it through the week.

Closeup lens gone: On older models, there is a lens located at the aperture of the camera. If it is missing, the projected image will be out of focus. Put the lens back on. Newer models do not have this problem.

Color switch on: On older models, if an exhibit is black and white—such as a document that has only black type on white paper—the color switch should be off. This will produce a sharper image. When an exhibit is in color—such as a photo or chart—the color switch needs to be turned back on. Newer models operate with the color switch on and do not have this problem.

Line in/line out problems: An evidence camera has a very simple pattern for hookup and the labels are clear. The evidence camera is putting OUT signals to the projector or monitors where images are going to be displayed. Therefore the cable from the evidence camera should be connected to the jack on the evidence camera labeled "line out." The projector or monitor is taking IN signals from the evidence camera; therefore the cable should be connected to the jack on the projector or monitor labeled "line in."

11.2.2 When things don't work

No image appears on the screen.

- Lens cap not removed
- Equipment not plugged in
- Output (to projector or monitors) not hooked up correctly

The image cannot be focused.

- The document is too dark or the object is too glowing
- Strong light is reflected on the screen

- An object has low contrast
- Focusing has been set in manual mode (try auto-focus)
- The "image freeze" feature is active (turn it off)

The zoom function does not work.

- The "image freeze" function is active. Turn it off.

The image on the screen appears reddish or bluish.

- The white balance has been adjusted manually (try auto-balance)

The image on the screen is too bright or too dark.

- The lighting is not correct (turn the upper lights on or off)
- The exposure setting is wrong (adjust the iris or exposure knob)

The image on the screen will not change.

- The "image freeze" function is active. Turn it off.

The upper lights do not light up right away when the on-button is pressed.

- There is a short "warm-up" period for these lamps. They will come on within 30 seconds.

Chapter 12: Technical Features, Manufacturers, and Specifications

This chapter covers the technical aspects of acquiring an evidence camera, whether by rental or purchase. The first section describes the principal features relevant to trial work. The second section provides information about manufacturers of evidence cameras and sources for further research. The third section provides comparative specifications for some of the more popular models. New models and capabilities come onto the market with some frequency, so it is a good idea to update the information here with a survey of the manufacturers' Web sites to see the most recent developments.

12.1 Desirable features

A wish list of features for an evidence camera to be used in a courtroom might include the following, set out in roughly the order of importance for trial work:

Digital equipment

For courtroom use, a digital evidence camera is generally better than analog equipment. Most courtroom users will want a digital projector or digital monitors for displaying the evidence camera's images. In addition, most users will want the evidence camera to operate in conjunction with a laptop computer, if not at the first technology-enabled trial, then soon thereafter. These other digital units are operated more easily with a digital evidence camera.

High resolution

Resolution is a measure of the quality of the image and the clarity with which details can be discerned. Most digital evidence cameras are capable of higher resolution than analog models. This is particularly important with respect to the display of documents. Most older evidence cameras cannot display a full page of print in a readable fashion, necessitating the use of the zoom feature to focus in on a part of the page. Newer digital models usually can display a full page in entirely readable fashion.

Manufacturers usually offer three specifications that affect full-page readability: the type of image sensor (1/2 inch or 1/3 inch CCD), the number of pixels, and the number of horizontal and vertical lines (eg. 1280 x 1024). In each case, more (bigger) is better.

High zoom capability

Evidence cameras have a wide range of zoom capability. Most that work well in the courtroom have 8x to 12x zoom power. More zoom provides larger magnification but not necessarily better images.

Freeze feature

The freeze feature allows the user to press a button and keep the image on the screen while the exhibit is removed from the base and another exhibit is placed on the base. This avoids distracting on-off movements picked up by the camera and blanks on the screen. It makes the courtroom presentation go more smoothly.

§12.1

Remote control (wireless)

A wireless remote control contains most of the buttons on the front panel and allows the user to operate the evidence camera while standing anywhere within 15 feet of the front of the unit. This flexibility means that the lawyer is not tied to the table where the evidence camera has been placed.

Document positioning indicators

Placing a document page on the evidence camera's base in the precisely correct position so that the image appears squarely on the screen is often difficult to do without positioning indicators. Evidence cameras with these positioning indicators are better for courtroom use.

Image memory

This feature allows the user to save several images for easy and quick retrieval at a later time. These images can show an entire exhibit or can be zoomed-in on a portion of an exhibit. With saved images, the lawyer does not have to put the document, photo, or object back on the base. These saved images can be created either before trial or can be saved as the trial proceeds. Counsel can thus identify images that will be used repeatedly and can summon them for use with witnesses or in opening and closing.

Automatic and manual image controls

There are three important controls that affect the quality of the image produced by the evidence camera.

The white balance controls ensure that only the proper amount of light enters the camera to maintain excellent image quality, which is important for documents with very small print.

The focus controls counter fuzzy images due to improper distance from the lens.

The exposure (iris) controls help with images that are too dark or too bright.

Automatic (built-in) controls that operate when the unit is turned on are very useful in a courtroom setting where there is minimal time to fiddle with the controls as each exhibit is put on the evidence camera base.

Manual controls are important, particularly with three-dimensional objects, when the automatic controls cannot capture just the right setting under ambient lighting in the courtroom.

Built-in backlight

A backlight in the base is needed if you want to display X-rays, CAT scans, MRI images, or other photographic negatives.

Scrolling

This capability eliminates the need to move the document or object on the base of the evidence camera.

Maneuverable retractable arm

A maneuverable arm supporting the camera is necessary in order to use the camera to capture images from locations in the courtroom other than the evidence camera's base. For example, training the camera on a whiteboard, blackboard, or flip chart can only be done if the camera is maneuverable.

A retractable arm allows the folded evidence camera to have a smaller footprint.

Support for external image sources

An evidence camera can be equipped to accept input from a laptop computer (playing a PowerPoint slide show), a VCR (playing videotapes), a still or motion digital camera. This allows an integrated presentation in the courtroom.

An input source switch on the base of the evidence camera allows quick and seamless change from one input source to another.

Flexibility in display resolutions

The resolution of the image that is output by the evidence camera must match or be lower than the resolution capability of the projector or monitor which will display the image.

Some evidence cameras have converters which allow them to convert to a lower resolution to accommodate a projector, monitor, or laptop with a lower resolution.

Scanning capability for objects

Occasionally an opponent may come up with a surprise object or scale model as an exhibit. One way to "copy" exhibits like this is to have an evidence camera with "scanning" capability. The evidence camera takes a picture (still or moving) of the exhibit, and the images are transferred to a laptop computer.

Foldable, portable design

An evidence camera that folds up and is highly portable makes courtroom support easier. The arm supporting the camera is retractable, and folds down on the base. The two wing or upper lights also fold down on the base. The unit should have a handle and a cover so that, once folded, it can be carried conveniently.

Light weight

It is helpful when the unit is relatively light weight, especially if the courtroom must be cleared every day.

12.2 Manufacturers

Most large suppliers of courtroom equipment, such as DOAR Communications, Inc., 170 Earle Avenue, Lynbrook, NY 11563, *www.doar.com*, carry evidence cameras optimized for courtroom use. Audio-visual rental companies also carry evidence cameras (which they often call document cameras or visual presenters).

The principal manufacturers of evidence cameras have developed digital models to supplement, and in some cases, replace their analog models. Developments in evidence camera technology were slow during the 1990s, but increased considerably with the addition of digital capability in 2000. The information set out in this section and the next section showing some comparative specifications is current as of January 2004.

One manufacturer, Toshiba, has a product that combines a portable digital projector with a digital evidence camera. This unit is particularly well-suited for courtroom use because it decreases the clutter and increases the flexibility of the setup in the courtroom.

AVerMedia
1161 Cadillac Court
Milpitas, CA 95035
Phone: 408-942-2121
Fax 408-263-8132
www.aver.com

AVerMedia is a Taiwan company founded in 1990, which opened a branch in the US in 1991. In addition to document cameras, it manufactures TV tuners, PC-to-TV converters, and digital photo viewers.

AVerMedia manufactures four document camera models:

AVerVision 300
AVerVision 280
AVerVision 110
AVerVision 100

Canon U.S.A., Inc.
NEW YORK OFFICE
One Canon Plaza,
Lake Success, NY 11042
Phone: 516-328-5960

LOS ANGELES OFFICE
15955 Alton Parkway
Irvine, CA 92718-3616
Phone: 714-753-4320
www.canonprojectors.com

Canon is a Japanese company founded in 1937. It manufactures copiers, printers, and fax machines, and cameras and optical equipment.

Canon manufactures three analog visualizers, the RE-450X, the RE-350, and the Vizcam 1000. Canon has one digital document camera, DZ-3600U.

ELMO Manufacturing Co.
1478 Old Country Road,
Plainview, NY 11803-5034
Phone: 516-501-1400
Fax. 516-501-0429
www.elmousa.com

ELMO is a Japanese company that specializes in products for the presentation of images, and has been in business since 1921. ELMO makes overhead projectors, film and slide projectors, and digital and analog visual presenters.

ELMO offers four analog and six digital visual presenters. The digital models are:

HV-8000SX

HV-7000SX

HV-5100XG

HV-5000XG

HV-3000XG

HV-100XG (small portable unit)

Epson America, Inc.
3840 Kilroy Airport Way,
Long Beach, CA 90806
www.epson.com

Epson is a Japanese company founded in 1942. It now has 111 companies under its corporate umbrella, and manufactures computers, peripherals, semiconductors, displays, and other equipment.

Epson manufactures three document cameras:

ELPDCO4: High resolution document camera

ELPDC03 Motion presentation camera

ELPDC02 High resolution document imager

Toshiba America, Inc.
Toshiba Display Devices, Inc.
100 Westinghouse Circle
Horseheads, NY 14845, U.S.A.
Tel: (607) 796-3500
Fax: (607) 796-3605
www.toshiba.com

Toshiba is a Japanese company founded in 1875. It now has 364 companies worldwide and manufactures information and communication systems, electronic components, heavy electrical apparatus, consumer products and medical imaging equipment.

Toshiba does not manufacture a separate document camera. It has three models of digital projectors that incorporate document cameras.

TLP-791U

TLP-T721U

TLP-T61MU

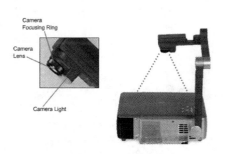

The TLP-T61 MU has a detachable document camera with an extension cable that allows you to place the document camera up to 9 feet from the projector.

12.3 Specifications

◆

This section sets out comparative specifications with respect to common features for one or two high-end models from the manufacturers with substantial presence in courtrooms. These tables include readily available published specifications. More detailed information and specifications for many of these models are available on the manufacturers' websites. Some models have additional capability as options; and manufacturers may have other models that include specific features not found in the listed models. This set of specifications provides the basic comparisons of capabilities; finer distinctions can be drawn with further research.

Other manufacturers also produce this equipment including WolfVision (Visualizer VZ-57), Samsung (Desktop Presenter SDP 6500) , JVC (Visual Presenter AV-P750U-DUK), Panasonic (Document Camera WE-MV180, and NEC (integrated projector and document camera DT20).

	AVerVision 300	AVerVision 280
Camera		
Lens	F2.8	F3.5
Shooting area		
Head rotation		
Image sensor	1/3-inch CCD	1/3-inch CCD
Pixels	850,000	790,000
Resolution	1024 x 768	1024 x 768
Zoom	8x	8x
Arm		
Length	22"	22"
Retractable	Yes	Yes
CBase controls		
Freeze	Yes	Yes
White balance	Auto/manual	Auto/manual
Focus		
Exposure	Auto/manual	Auto/manual
Rotate	Yes (180°)	Yes (180°)
Flip/mirror	Yes	Yes
Neg/pos	Yes	Yes
Color/BW	Yes	Yes
Scroll		
On screen menu	Yes	Yes
Remote control	Yes	No
Video pointer		
Lighting		
Upper		
Backlight	Yes (oOptional)	Yes (optional)
Document pos.	Yes LED	Yes LED (optional)
Input/output		
RGB	DVI	Yes
Video	Yes	
S-Video		
RS-232C		
USB		
Audio		
Downconverter		
Input source switch	Yes	Yes
Image memory		
Image capture		
Portable		
Size (folded) (WxDxH)	8.8 x 5.6 x 2.2	8.8 x 5.6 x 2.2
Weight	3.9 lbs.	3.7 lbs
Power source		
Price (retail)	$999	$738

	Canon DZ-3600U	Canon RE 450X
Camera		
Lens	F1.8-2.8	F1.8 – 2.8
Shooting area	13.2 x 9.9	12.75 x 9.5
Head rotation	Yes	
Image sensor	1/3-inch CCD	1/3-inch CCD
Pixels	410,000	850,000
Resolution	1900 x 1424	1024 x 768 XGA
Zoom	12x	12x
Arm		
Length		
Retractable	Yes	
CBase controls		
Freeze		Yes
White balance	Auto/manual	Auto/manual
Focus	Auto/manual	Auto/manual
Exposure	Auto/manual	Auto/manual
Rotate	Yes	
Flip/mirror	Yes	
Neg/pos	Yes	
Color/BW	Yes	
Scroll	Yes	
On screen menu		
Remote control	Yes	Yes
Video pointer		
Lighting		
Upper	6W fluorescent	6W fluorescent
Backlight	6W fluorescent	4.8W cold cathode
Document pos.		
Input/output		
RGB		Yes
Video	Yes	Yes
S-Video	Yes	Yes
RS-232C	Yes	Yes
USB	Yes	
Audio		
Downconverter		Yes
Input source switch		Yes
Image memory		
Image capture	Yes	
Portable		
Size (folded) (WxDxH)	19.1 x 20.7 x 8.1	19 x 20.5 x 7.2
Weight	22 lbs	22 lbs
Power source	AC 120V	AC 200-240V
Price (retail)	$3,918	$1,795

§12.3

	Elmo HV-8000SX	Elmo HV-5100 SX
Camera		
Lens	F2.8	F2.8
Shooting area	14.3 x 11.4	13.7 x 10.2
Head rotation	Yes (180°)	
Image sensor	1/2-inch CCD	1/3-inch CCD
Pixels	1,500,000	850,000
Resolution	1280 x 1024 SXGA	1024 x 768 XGA
Zoom	10x	18x
Arm		
Length		
Retractable	Yes	Yes
CBase controls		
Freeze	Yes	Yes
White balance	Auto/manual	Auto/manual
Focus	Auto/manual	Auto/manual
Exposure	Auto	Auto/manual
Rotate	Yes (180°)	Yes
Flip/mirror		
Neg/pos	Yes	Yes
Color/BW	Yes	Yes
Scroll	Yes	Yes
On screen menu	Yes	Yes
Remote control	Yes (also location)	Yes
Video pointer	Yes	Yes
Lighting		
Upper	Fluorescent	6W fluorescent
Backlight	Yes	Yes
Document pos.		
Input/output		
RGB	Yes	Yes
Video	Yes	Yes
S-Video	Yes	Yes
RS-232C	Yes	Yes
USB	Yes	Yes
Audio	Yes	Yes
Downconverter	Built in	Yes
Input source switch		
Image memory		Yes (8)
Image capture	Yes	
Portable		
Size (folded) (WxDxH)	21 x 17.7 x 7.3	15.8 x 21.3 x 7.1
Weight	23.2 lbs	21.6 lbs.
Power source	AC 100-240V	AC 100-240V
Price (retail)	$4,615	$2,615

	Epson ELPDCO4	Epson ELPDC02
Camera		
Lens	F2.8	F2.8
Shooting area	13.4 x 9.9	14.0 x 10.4
Head rotation	Yes	
Image sensor	1/3-inch CCD	1/3-inch CCD
Pixels	850,000	850,000
Resolution	1024 x 768	1024 x 768
Zoom	10x	10x
Arm		
Length		
Retractable	No	No
CBase controls		
Freeze	Yes	
White balance	Auto/manual	Auto
Focus	Auto/manual	Auto/manual
Exposure	Auto/manual	Auto/manual
Rotate		
Flip/mirror		
Neg/pos		
Color/BW	Yes	
Scroll		
On screen menu	Yes	
Remote control	Yes	Yes
Video pointer	Yes	
Lighting		
Upper	9W fluorescent	6W fluorescent
Backlight		Yes
Document pos.		
Input/output		
RGB	Yes	Yes
Video	Yes	Yes
S-Video		Yes
RS-232C	Yes	Yes
USB	Yes	
Audio		
Downconverter		
Input source switch		Yes
Image memory		
Image capture	Yes	
Portable		
Size (folded) (WxDxH)	19.7 x 24.1 x 3.9	16 x 26.4 x 6.7
Weight	14.3 lbs.	22.1 lbs.
Power source	AC 100-120V	AC 100-120V
Price (retail)	$1,812	$1,844

	Toshiba TLP-791U	Toshiba TLP-721U
Camera		
Lens	F3.1	F2.8
Shooting area		
Head rotation	Yes	
Image sensor	½ inch CCD	1/3 inch CCD
Pixels	1,447,680	810,000
Resolution	1024 x 768 XGA	1024 x 768 XGA
Zoom	10x	
Arm		
Length		
Retractable	Yes	Yes
Controls		
Freeze		
White balance	Manual	Manual
Focus	Manual	Manual
Exposure	Manual	Manual
Rotate		
Flip/mirror		
Neg/pos		
Color/BW		
Scroll		
On screen menu		
Remote control	Yes	Yes
Video pointer	Yes (plus overlay)	Yes (plus overlay)
Lighting		
Upper	Yes (under camera)	Yes (under camera)
Backlight	No	No
Document pos.	No	No
Input/output		
RGB	Yes	Yes
Video	Yes	Yes
S-Video		Yes
RS-232C	Yes	Yes
USB	Yes	Yes
Audio	Yes	Yes
Downconverter	Yes	Yes
Input source switch	Yes	Yes
Image memory		Yes
Image capture		Yes
Portable		
Size (folded) (WxDxH)	13.3 x 12.7 x 3.9	11.7 x 12.3 x 3.8
Weight	11.0 lbs.	9.0 lbs.
Power source	AC 100-240	AC 100-240
Price (retail)	$4,699	$3,999